The AI-Powered Wallet: Digital Wealth Management

A Practical Guide to Using AI and Tech for Smart Money Management,

ALEX SUTTON

Disclaimer

This book, *The AI-Powered Wallet: Digital Wealth Management*, is intended to provide general information and insights about leveraging artificial intelligence and financial technology for personal finance. The content is presented for educational purposes only and should not be construed as specific financial, investment, legal, or tax advice. While the authors and publishers have made every effort to ensure the accuracy and completeness of the information in this book, no guarantee is given regarding its applicability to individual circumstances, and the information may change as technology and financial markets evolve.

Readers are encouraged to consult with qualified financial, legal, or tax professionals before making any financial decisions based on the ideas and tools discussed in this book. The use of any AI-driven financial tools, apps, or investment platforms mentioned herein should be done with careful consideration and personal due diligence, and readers should be aware that these tools may carry inherent risks.

The authors and publishers disclaim any liability for direct or indirect loss, damage, or consequences arising from the use of, or reliance on, information in this book.

Contents

Foreword: Embracing the AI Revolution in Finance

Imagine this: it's the year 2035, and you're in a coffee shop. The barista hands you a latte made precisely to your taste preferences, not because you ordered it that way, but because an AI-driven app synced with your bank account noticed you've been stressed lately and figured you could use a pick-me-up. Oh, and this app also reminded you to save $3.75 because, well, every cent counts.

If that sounds too far-fetched, let me assure you, we're already heading there.

The world of personal finance has shifted dramatically in recent years. Long gone are the days of balancing check books (remember those?). Today, AI doesn't just "manage" your finances—it predicts, suggests, negotiates, and saves without so much as a nudge. For many of us, our wallets now have minds of their own. Whether that sounds exhilarating or a bit unnerving, it's the new reality, and it's here to stay.

So why a book about AI and your money? Because, let's face it, most of us don't have the time—or let's be real, the patience—to keep up with all the shiny new tools promising to make us millionaires by next Tuesday. This book isn't about flashy promises; it's about practical ways you can use technology right now to make, save, and grow money with less effort and more efficiency. Think of it as your roadmap to understanding and leveraging tech to give your financial life a boost, no matter where you're starting from.

I've written this book because I believe we're at a tipping point: those who understand how to integrate AI into their finances will find themselves financially empowered, while those who ignore it might get left behind. Not so long ago, I realized this myself after a quick check on my "smart wallet" app (yes, that's a thing now) revealed I'd been paying for four—yes, four!—streaming services I barely used. A few clicks later, my subscriptions were trimmed, and my AI app had set up a mini savings plan with the newfound "extra" cash. Small victories like this may seem minor, but they're part of a bigger transformation.

Whether you're a tech geek, a finance newbie, or just someone looking to save a bit more cash month, this book will show you how to turn AI from an abstract buzzword into a personal financial advisor that's accessible, reliable, and maybe even a little bit fun.

AI won't magically make us all billionaires, but it can give us tools that are smarter, faster, and maybe even a little cheekier than traditional finance ever was. You'll learn about budgeting apps that know your spending patterns better than you do, robo-advisors that adjust your investments while you sleep, and even AI-driven platforms that make growing wealth feel as easy as swiping on a dating app (just with a little less heartbreak).

So, get comfortable and maybe grab a coffee—AI didn't order it for you just yet. You're about to take a journey through the future of finance, and it's one that I promise will leave you feeling both excited and prepared for what's coming. In this brave new world, your wallet is smart, your money is managed, and you're in control—no spreadsheet necessary.

Welcome to the AI revolution. Your financial future just got a serious upgrade.

DIY Financial Health Check

This DIY Financial Health Check is designed to give you a quick, honest snapshot of your current financial situation. Answer the following questions to identify areas where AI-driven tools could help you improve. After you complete the check, use the recommended chapters as a guide to deepen your understanding and get personalized support in the areas that need the most attention.

Section 1: Budgeting & Expense Tracking
Questions:

1. Do you currently have a monthly budget that you follow?
   - Yes, I follow it closely.
   - I have one, but I don't track it very well.
   - No, I don't currently use a budget.
2. How often do you review and categorize your spending?
   - Weekly or monthly
   - Occasionally
   - Rarely or never

3. Do you know what percentage of your income you're spending on essentials, entertainment, and savings each month?
    - Yes
    - Kind of
    - No

If you answered mostly "No" or "Rarely," consider exploring: *Chapter 7: AI-Driven Budgeting and Expense Tracking*

Section 2: Saving & Emergency Fund Questions:

1. Do you have an emergency fund with 3-6 months' worth of living expenses?
    - Yes, I have a fully funded emergency fund.
    - I'm working on it but not quite there.
    - No, I haven't started yet.
2. How regularly are you able to set aside money for savings?
    - Every paycheck
    - Occasionally
    - Rarely or never
3. Are you using any automated tools or apps to help you save consistently?
    - Yes, and it's working well for me.
    - I'm using some tools, but I'm not consistent.
    - No, I don't automate my savings.

If you answered mostly "No" or "Rarely," consider exploring: *Chapter 8: Smarter Shopping with AI* and *Chapter 9: Optimizing Bills and Reducing Debt with AI*

Section 3: Debt Management
Questions:

1. Are you currently managing any high-interest debt (e.g., credit cards, personal loans)?
    - No, I'm debt-free or paying off low-interest debt.
    - Yes, but I have a solid plan to pay it off.
    - Yes, and it feels unmanageable.
2. Do you know your interest rates, monthly payments, and payoff timelines?
    - Yes, I know the details of each debt.
    - I have some idea, but not everything.
    - No, I'm not sure about these details.
3. Are you using any AI-driven tools to help you track and manage debt repayment?
    - Yes, and it's helping me stay on top of things.
    - I've tried, but I haven't found the right tool yet.
    - No, I'm not using any tools.

If you answered mostly "Yes, and it feels unmanageable," or "No," consider exploring: *Chapter 9: Optimizing Bills and Reducing Debt with AI*

Section 4: Investment Knowledge & Strategy
Questions:

1. Are you currently investing in the stock market, real estate, or other asset classes?
    - Yes, I have a diverse portfolio.
    - Yes, but it's limited (mostly in one type of asset).
    - No, I'm not investing yet.
2. Do you have a clear investment strategy based on your financial goals and risk tolerance?

- Yes, I have a strategy that I follow.
    - I have a general idea but could use more structure.
    - No, I haven't developed a strategy.
3. Are you comfortable with the risks associated with your current investments?
    - Yes, I understand my portfolio and its risks.
    - Mostly, but I could use more clarity.
    - No, I'm not fully sure about the risks.

If you answered mostly "No" or "I could use more clarity," consider exploring: *Chapter 10: Building a Diverse Portfolio with AI Assistance* and *Chapter 11: Personalized Financial Advice and Wealth Management*

Section 5: Retirement Goals & Long-Term Planning Questions:

1. Have you set specific retirement goals (age, income needs, lifestyle, etc.)?
    - Yes, I have clear goals for retirement.
    - I have some idea but haven't fully defined them.
    - No, I haven't thought much about it.
2. Do you know how much you should be saving each month to reach your retirement goals?
    - Yes, I have a calculated amount.
    - I have a rough estimate, but not an exact amount.
    - No, I haven't calculated it.
3. Are you using any tools to help track progress toward retirement?
    - Yes, and I find them helpful.
    - I've tried some, but they didn't work for me.
    - No, I'm not using any tools.

If you answered mostly "No" or "I haven't thought much about it," consider exploring: *Chapter 12: Preparing for the Future: Retirement and Long-Term Financial Planning*

Results and Next Steps

After answering the questions, review the chapters that correspond to your "No" or "Rarely" responses to focus on the areas where AI-driven tools could be especially useful. Here's a quick summary to guide you:

- **If you need help with Budgeting**: Go to *Chapter 7: AI-Driven Budgeting and Expense Tracking*
- **If you want to improve your Saving habits**: Check out *Chapter 8: Smarter Shopping with AI*
- **If Debt Management is a priority**: Dive into *Chapter 9: Optimizing Bills and Reducing Debt with AI*
- **If you're interested in Investments**: Explore *Chapter 10: Building a Diverse Portfolio with AI Assistance*
- **For Retirement Planning**: Focus on *Chapter 12: Preparing for the Future: Retirement and Long-Term Financial Planning*

Use this Financial Health Check as a starting point to identify which chapters—and tools—will provide the most immediate value to you. Remember, personal finance is a journey, and AI tools can help you make meaningful progress step by step.

Part One

Understanding the AI-Driven Financial Landscape

Chapter 1
The New Era of Money Management

Let's start with a question: when was the last time you walked into an actual bank branch? Or called your bank for anything other than to dispute that mysterious late-night pizza order? If you're like most people, it's probably been a while. In the last decade, financial technology—affectionately known as "fintech"—has taken the world by storm, transforming the way we handle, view, and even think about money. And now, at the center of this revolution, artificial intelligence is rewriting the rules of personal finance.

A Quick Look at Fintech's Rocket-Fueled Rise

Just a few decades ago, the biggest innovation in banking was the invention of ATMs. No more standing in line to withdraw cash or deposit checks! But fast-forward to today, and we have budgeting apps that track our spending habits better than we do, robo-advisors that automatically invest our money, and digital wallets that let us leave our wallets at home. Whether it's splitting bills, transferring funds, or checking your credit score, fintech has made everything simpler, faster, and mobile.

But fintech alone wasn't enough. As the field matured, we started to see a whole new layer added on top—artificial intelligence. If fintech put our money into our hands, AI is now shaping what we do with it.

How AI is Shaking Up the Financial World

So, what exactly is AI doing to our finances? Well, imagine a world where your bank account actively tries to keep you from overspending on yet another overpriced latte. Or where your investment portfolio can automatically rebalance based on both market trends and your own risk tolerance, all while you're busy binge-watching your favorite show. In short, AI doesn't just take on repetitive financial tasks—it learns from them, adjusts for your preferences, and gives you real-time insights to make better money decisions.

Let's break it down a little further. Here are some real ways AI is impacting the financial industry:

1. **AI-Powered Personal Assistants**: Imagine Siri or Alexa, but for your money. Financial apps and banks are now offering AI-powered virtual assistants that can help you check your balance, track your spending, and even set up savings goals. For example, Bank of America's "Erica" and Capital One's "Eno" are already in action, helping customers manage their money with a simple tap or voice command. They're basically the money-savvy best friends we never knew we needed.

2. **Robo-Advisors**: These are AI-driven investment platforms that manage your investments for you. Gone are the days when you needed a human advisor to tell you where to put your money. Robo-advisors analyze the market, assess your risk tolerance, and make investment

decisions on your behalf, often with lower fees and minimums than traditional advisors. Think of it like having your own personal Wall Street expert—minus the pinstripe suit and thousand-dollar fees.

3. **AI in Credit Scoring**: Believe it or not, AI is also helping reshape how credit scores are determined. Traditional credit scoring relies heavily on credit history and doesn't account for things like your actual ability to pay bills on time. Newer AI-driven scoring models can look at a broader set of factors, from your regular expenses to how much you save each month, making credit more accessible to people with thin credit files.

4. **Fraud Detection**: One of AI's most crucial roles in finance is spotting suspicious activity in real time. AI algorithms can flag a potential fraud attempt far faster than humans can. So if someone tries to buy 12 designer handbags on your card while you're napping, there's a good chance your bank's AI system will step in to save the day.

5. **Automated Budgeting and Savings**: Ever heard of apps like Digit or Qapital? These use AI to help you save by analyzing your spending habits and automatically moving small amounts into savings. Sometimes, these apps are so good that you'll forget you're saving at all—until you check your account and find that you've stashed away enough for a mini-vacation or a new gadget. AI-driven budgeting has made managing money feel almost effortless.

Why AI-Driven Money Management Matters for Young Professionals

Young professionals today face a unique financial landscape: they're likely to have student debt, a high cost of living, and a job market that demands flexibility. Balancing all this can be overwhelming. AI can make it easier by taking on the repetitive (and often time-consuming) aspects of personal finance. And because AI learns from your financial behavior, it can also give you insights and recommendations that feel surprisingly relevant—sometimes even eerily so.

AI doesn't just help you "manage" money; it can transform your relationship with it. Instead of spending hours logging every expense, you can use an AI app to do the heavy lifting for you. Instead of manually rebalancing your investment portfolio, a robo-advisor can handle it based on market conditions. And instead of having to remember to set aside savings each month, an AI-powered tool can do it in the background, almost like magic.

AI tools are invaluable for young professionals not just because they save time but because they offer a way to build financial confidence. Let's face it: finance can be intimidating, especially if you're new to it. The technical terms, the complex graphs, the sheer number of decisions—it's a lot to handle. AI simplifies that. It gives you insights that help you feel informed and in control without needing to be a finance expert.

Funny Facts and Real Truths About AI in Finance

Let's pause for a second to appreciate the fact that AI isn't just some disembodied software. It has a personality—a quirky, data-driven personality, but a personality nonetheless. For example, there are reports of budgeting apps that'll nudge you with guilt-inducing notifications when you spend too much on dining out (because maybe you really don't need that third delivery order this week). Other apps gamify saving money, sending you virtual high-fives for sticking to your budget. Some people even say their budgeting app "roasts" them when they splurge on something unnecessary. It's like having a financially responsible friend who's not afraid to call you out!

On a more serious note, though, all these nudges, reminders, and real-time data help us do what generations before us couldn't: track every dollar and make sure it's working for us. AI can guide us to financial success by helping us stick to budgets, save more efficiently, and invest wisely.

A Future Where AI and Finances Go Hand in Hand

The new era of money management is only just beginning. With AI at the helm, the future of finance looks exciting, efficient, and, yes, just a little bit witty. Young professionals who get on board with this technology now will be better prepared for the financial world of tomorrow—a world where managing your money doesn't feel like a chore but like an extension of your daily routine.

So, the next time you check your balance, think about what's happening behind the scenes. You're not just seeing a number. You're interacting with a technology that's learning, predicting, and protecting your financial well-being. And this is only the start. AI isn't here to take over your money; it's here to help you take control, one algorithm at a time.

Chapter 2
Core Concepts – AI, Machine Learning, and Personal Finance

I f AI and machine learning sound intimidating, don't worry; we're not here to turn you into a data scientist. We're here to demystify these buzzwords, show how they can work for you, and, most importantly, make sense of why they matter to your wallet.

What is AI, and Why Should You Care?

Artificial intelligence, or AI, is essentially the creation of systems that can "think" and "learn" like humans. Instead of programming a computer to perform a single, specific task, AI can adapt, learn, and improve over time based on data—think of it like having a hyper-efficient assistant who remembers everything and is always on the lookout for ways to optimize your life.

Machine learning (ML) is the driving engine behind AI. It's a subset of AI that involves feeding machines massive amounts of data so they can find patterns, make predictions, and even make decisions based on what they learn. Imagine a toddler learning that fire is hot after getting too close a few times; ML algorithms learn through a similar process, minus the ouch factor.

To put it simply, while traditional programming is like teaching a dog to fetch, AI and ML are like giving the dog the ability to analyze and fetch every stick with minimal training. And as it turns out, AI and ML are fantastic at handling repetitive, data-driven tasks—which is why they're perfect for personal finance.

Key AI-Driven Tools in Personal Finance

AI and ML are more than just fascinating concepts; they're practical, everyday tools that are here to make personal finance more manageable, accurate, and accessible. Here are some of the real MVPs (Most Valuable Programs) making waves in personal finance.

1. Budgeting Apps: Your Automated Money Whisperer

If you've ever wondered why your budget seems to vanish into thin air after a few nights out or an online shopping spree, meet your new best friends: AI-powered budgeting apps like **Mint**, **YNAB (You Need a Budget)**, and **PocketGuard**. These apps use machine learning to analyze your spending patterns, track where your money is going, and even categorize purchases to help you see what's eating up your budget.

For example, PocketGuard doesn't just show you what you spent; it tells you what's "safe to spend" based on your bills, expenses, and savings goals. Imagine a money-savvy friend whispering in your ear, "Hey, maybe skip that extra guac today." AI-driven budgeting apps like these track not only where your money has gone but also predict where it might go—helping you keep more of it in your pocket.

Real Life Example

Take Mint, for instance. Not only does it track your expenses, but it also provides alerts if you're nearing the limit on a category you've been splurging on, like dining out. You'd be surprised how much a "maybe skip that latte" notification can save over a month. According to a study by Intuit (Mint's parent company), regular users of Mint saved an average of $200 per month just by tracking and making conscious spending choices. That's $2,400 a year back in your pocket with almost no effort!

2. Robo-Advisors: Your Virtual Investment Coach

Robo-advisors sound like they might wear a little bow tie and spout investment jargon, but they're actually digital platforms that help you invest money, usually at a lower cost than traditional financial advisors. Companies like **Betterment**, **Wealthfront**, and **Ellevest** use algorithms to create and manage a diversified investment portfolio tailored to your goals, risk tolerance, and timeline. And the best part? They do it automatically.

Robo-advisors are trained with historical data to make sound investment choices for you, balancing your portfolio as market conditions change, so you don't have to. They're especially appealing to young professionals who don't have time (or maybe interest) in managing a portfolio manually but still want to see their money grow.

Real Life Example

Let's talk about Wealthfront, one of the pioneers in the robo-advisor space. Wealthfront doesn't just invest your money and call it a day; it also offers a service called "Tax-Loss Harvesting," which strategically sells and repurchases assets to minimize the taxes you pay. According to Wealthfront's own research, tax-loss harvesting can boost a portfolio's annual returns by about 1-2%. Over time, that could translate into thousands of extra dollars—without you lifting a finger or even knowing what tax-loss harvesting means.

3. AI-Enhanced Investment Platforms: Smarter Trading with Data

Investment platforms like **Acorns** and **Robinhood** have made investing as easy as ordering a pizza, and some of them have integrated AI to make the process even smarter. Acorns, for instance, rounds up your purchases and invests the spare change, turning your coffee habit into an investment portfolio. On top of that, it uses algorithms to balance and rebalance your portfolio automatically, so you don't have to play stock market guru.

Robinhood also offers data-driven insights into which stocks are trending, letting you see the "mood" of the market at a glance. This is especially handy for new investors who want a starting point but might not know where to begin.

Real Life Example

With Acorns, every time you make a purchase, it rounds up the amount to the nearest dollar and invests the change. Over a year, those nickels and dimes add up. According to Acorns, the average user invests about $166 a month just through round-ups—money that would otherwise just vanish from our wallets. For people who struggle to save, this micro-saving, micro-investing feature is a game-changer.

How AI Tools Make Financial Management More Accessible and Accurate

So, what's the big deal? Why is AI such a powerful tool for personal finance? Well, for one thing, AI has no human hang-ups. It doesn't have an off-day, it doesn't procrastinate, and it doesn't avoid looking at bank statements the way many of us do.

Removing the Guesswork

AI tools in personal finance remove much of the guesswork from money management. Algorithms can predict spending patterns, suggest ways to save, and even alert you to upcoming bills. AI systems look at data—lots of it—draw patterns from that data, and make recommendations based on what it learns. In fact, some AI-driven budgeting apps are so good at identifying your spending habits that they'll know what you're likely to spend on in advance, helping you make smarter decisions.

Taking the Emotion Out of Money

One of the biggest challenges of personal finance is that money is, well, personal. We've all made those impulsive purchases, whether it's a "just because" treat or a "treat yourself" shopping spree. AI isn't swayed by emotions or the urge to buy that 12th pair of shoes. It takes a purely data-driven approach, making it an impartial, unbiased money manager that has only one goal: to help you achieve your financial objectives.

Helping Those New to Finance

Let's be honest—finance can feel like a foreign language, especially when you're just starting out. AI-powered tools can make it less intimidating, offering tips and guidance without judgment. Budgeting apps can flag your spending without saying, "Maybe you should rethink that gym membership you're not using." And robo-advisors can help you invest without a background in finance, making it easier for anyone to get started.

Making Financial Management "Invisible"

With the right AI-powered tools, a lot of money management can happen without you even realizing it. Auto-saving, auto-investing, and even auto-rebalancing all happen in the background, leaving you more time for, well, anything else. The best AI tools take care of things behind the scenes, and many people find this level of automation to be a relief—one less thing on a very long to-do list.

Final Thoughts: AI and the Democratization of Finance

The beauty of AI in personal finance is that it levels the playing field. A budgeting app doesn't care if you're managing millions or living paycheck-to-paycheck; it's there to help you get the most out of your money. Robo-advisors make investing possible without the hefty fees, and AI-enhanced credit scoring can help people qualify for loans who might otherwise struggle to do so.

By making financial management more accessible, AI empowers people to take control of their finances in ways that weren't possible even a decade ago. The barriers to entry have lowered, and now anyone with a smartphone can manage, save, and grow their money—no finance degree or investment banker required.

In this new era, the only requirement is a willingness to let technology work for you. So why not give AI a shot? The future of finance isn't about making you a robot—it's about giving you the tools you need to take charge of your financial future. And thanks to AI, those tools are just a few taps away.

Chapter 3
The Rise of Smart Wallets and Digital Banking

L et's face it: most of us would rather dive into a shark tank than stand in line at a bank. And luckily, thanks to the digital revolution, we don't have to. Banking has undergone a serious transformation over the past decade. Those lines, those tellers, those endless forms... they're becoming relics of a bygone era, like Blockbuster and pagers. In their place, we have digital-first banking and "smart wallets"—AI-powered digital companions that fit snugly in our phones and are ready to help manage our money whenever we need.

Welcome to the era of smart wallets and digital banking, where you can handle almost every banking task without ever touching a bank branch. Let's take a look at how we got here and why these tools are changing the way we manage our money.

From Brick-and-Mortar to Bits-and-Bytes: The Shift to Digital Banking

Once upon a time, if you needed to cash a check or open a savings account, you had to trek down to your local bank. This was a process involving long waits, a lot of paperwork, and—let's be honest —awkward small talk. But as technology evolved, banks began shifting their focus to digital services, realizing that their customers were much happier managing their money from the comfort of their couches.

Today, "digital-first" banks, also known as **neobanks** or **challenger banks**, are entirely online. Banks like **Chime**, **Ally**, and **Revolut** offer everything from checking and savings accounts to investment options—all without a single physical branch. And people love it. A survey by FIS in 2021 found that 70% of people preferred digital channels to physical branches for banking. And who can blame them? When was the last time you heard someone say, "I just love waiting in line"?

But it's not just about convenience. Digital banking allows for seamless integration with other apps and services, lets us access banking features 24/7, and often comes with lower fees since these banks don't have to maintain costly physical locations. In other words, digital banking is not only easier but often cheaper. What's not to like?

The Magic of Digital Wallets: Paying Without the Hassle

Digital wallets have taken this revolution one step further by making actual wallets optional. **Apple Pay**, **Google Wallet**, **PayPal**, and **Samsung Pay** are a few of the big players that allow us to pay for almost anything without ever reaching for cash or a card. Just wave your phone, and voilà—payment complete.

For those new to digital wallets, here's a breakdown of how they work: you link your bank account, credit, or debit card to the app. The app then stores your card details securely and lets you use it to pay with a tap. The transaction is encrypted, making it safer than traditional magnetic stripe cards (sorry, old-school credit card skimmers!). Digital wallets even offer added layers of security, like fingerprint recognition or face ID, so if your phone takes a solo journey, no one can get to your financial info.

But digital wallets aren't just about payments. They also help track your spending, store loyalty rewards, manage subscriptions, and even find deals or discounts. They've become so popular that, according to a study by Juniper Research, the number of people using digital wallets worldwide will exceed 4.4 billion by 2025. Digital wallets are transforming how we pay and what we carry. Imagine the extra pocket space!

What is a Smart Wallet, Anyway?

If digital wallets made your wallet digital, **smart wallets** are taking it one step further: they're digital wallets infused with artificial intelligence. Unlike a digital wallet that simply stores your cards and processes payments, a smart wallet can analyze your spending, give you tailored budgeting advice, offer investment insights, and even remind you of upcoming bills—all without you lifting a finger.

Think of it as a financial assistant with a slight obsession for staying on top of your accounts. Smart wallets like **Emma**, **True-bill (now Rocket Money)**, and **Monzo** use AI to go beyond just storing your cards. They're designed to learn your financial habits and help you make better financial decisions by serving up alerts, recommendations, and personalized insights in real time.

Key Features of an AI-Powered Smart Wallet

1. **Spending Insights and Budgeting Suggestions**
2. Smart wallets can analyze your spending patterns and suggest areas where you can save. For example, if Emma notices you're spending a little too much on dining out (maybe three sushi orders in one week?), it'll send a nudge suggesting you might want to dial it down a notch.

It's like having an accountability partner—without the judgmental sighs.

3. **Real Life Example**

4. The Emma app, also dubbed "your best financial friend," analyzes transactions from all linked accounts and categorizes them. It'll spot irregularities, suggest savings goals, and even break down spending into handy charts. According to reviews, users report they've saved between $500 and $1,000 annually just by following Emma's nudges. And yes, Emma has been known to "roast" users a bit when they go overboard, which can be surprisingly effective!

5. **Automated Bill Tracking and Subscription Management**

6. Many of us are guilty of signing up for free trials that turn into "I totally forgot I was paying for this" subscriptions. Smart wallets have that covered. Apps like Rocket Money scan your account for recurring payments and even alert you to subscriptions you might want to cancel. They'll also remind you about upcoming bills so you don't end up with a late fee and a financial guilt trip.

7. **Real Life Example**

8. Rocket Money (formerly Truebill) helps users identify and cancel forgotten subscriptions. According to Rocket Money, the average user saves $512 per year by canceling unused subscriptions. One user reported that Rocket Money even negotiated their cable bill down by $120 a year. That's right—AI can help you haggle!

9. **Goal-Based Savings and Automated Micro-Investing**

10. Smart wallets often come with features that let you set savings goals and make progress toward them without thinking too much about it. Some, like **Qapital**, even let you set "rules" to automate savings in fun ways. For

instance, every time you hit your daily step goal, Qapital can transfer $5 into your vacation fund, or whenever you order takeout, it can set aside a few bucks for future savings.

11. **Acorns** takes this concept further by rounding up your everyday purchases to the nearest dollar and investing the spare change. While a few cents here and there may not sound like much, over time it can add up, especially when invested. According to Acorns, their average user invests $166 a month just through round-ups.

12. **Real-Time Fraud Detection and Security**

13. Smart wallets don't just keep your money; they protect it. With AI-powered algorithms that can detect suspicious activity, these apps act as an early warning system for fraud. Some apps even allow you to lock and unlock your card instantly if something looks fishy, all from your phone.

14. For example, digital bank **Monzo** is known for its proactive fraud detection. If Monzo's system suspects a transaction is fraudulent, it alerts the user immediately and temporarily freezes the card. The app even has a "Freeze Card" button, which lets users lock their card in seconds if they suspect foul play. In a world where card details can be compromised with a single wrong click, having real-time fraud detection is a game-changer.

15. **Financial Advice Tailored to Your Spending Habits**

16. Smart wallets don't just track—they advise. If you're overspending in one area, they'll let you know (with as much or as little sass as the app allows). If you're doing well on your budget, they'll encourage you to save even more. This personalized approach, powered by machine learning, makes AI-powered wallets feel like a friend who knows your finances inside and out.

Why Smart Wallets Matter: More Than Just a Trend

Smart wallets and digital banking are about more than just making transactions more convenient. They represent a fundamental shift in how we interact with our finances. Instead of passively tracking our spending, we're actively managing it. Instead of dreading budgeting, we're automating it. And instead of wondering where our money went, we know exactly where it's going—and we can adjust in real time.

For young professionals especially, smart wallets offer a way to stay on top of finances without getting overwhelmed. In a fast-paced, digital world, they provide the structure and support to help people make informed financial decisions, even if they're new to managing money.

Final Thoughts: The Future of Your Wallet is Digital

With AI and digital banking, the days of crumpled receipts and forgotten subscriptions are behind us. Smart wallets and digital-first banks are making it easier than ever to track, manage, and grow our money—all from our phones. And as these technologies continue to improve, they're likely to become even smarter, predicting our needs and helping us make better decisions with minimal effort.

In this new era of money management, your wallet doesn't just hold your cash; it's a digital partner that's always looking out for your financial well-being. Whether you're trying to save a little more each month, get rid of hidden subscriptions, or invest your spare change, there's a smart wallet ready to help.

The question is, are you ready to let it?

Part Two

Making Money with AI-Powered Tools

Chapter 4
Exploring AI-Powered Income Opportunities

In the age of AI, making money is no longer just about having a 9-to-5 job or even a steady side hustle. Now, technology is opening up a world of income opportunities that didn't exist just a few years ago. From gig economy jobs that make use of AI-powered platforms to content creation tools that can automate parts of your workflow, the possibilities are extensive—and the earnings potential can be, too.

This chapter is all about using AI to expand your income streams and explore new ways to bring in cash, whether you're looking to diversify your revenue or dive into a brand-new field.

The Gig Economy 2.0: AI-Powered Platforms for Side Hustles

The gig economy exploded with the rise of platforms like Uber, DoorDash, and TaskRabbit, which made it easy to work flexible hours and pick up jobs on the side. But the AI-powered gig economy has added another layer of innovation. New platforms are using AI to match workers with tasks, optimize routes, manage schedules, and even set competitive pricing—all designed to make gig work easier and more profitable.

Rideshare and Delivery Jobs: AI as Your Personal Dispatcher

If you're driving for a rideshare or delivery service, AI has likely become your silent partner. For example, **Uber** uses machine learning to predict where demand will be highest, helping drivers position themselves in busy areas. AI also assists in setting surge pricing based on real-time demand, meaning drivers can earn more during peak hours. **DoorDash**uses similar technology to match drivers with orders, while optimizing routes to maximize delivery efficiency.

While these platforms don't guarantee an income, they do offer flexibility and use AI to improve efficiency. According to a study by the JPMorgan Chase Institute, people who drive for rideshare services can earn an additional $300 to $500 per month on average. Not bad for a flexible side hustle that can be scheduled around other commitments.

AI-Driven Task Platforms: Virtual Assistance and Beyond

Platforms like **TaskRabbit** and **Fiverr** now use AI to help freelancers find jobs that match their skills and availability. AI isn't just working in the background; it's also handling everything from scheduling and task assignment to pricing suggestions, making these platforms much easier to navigate for freelancers and taskers alike.

Fiverr, for example, uses machine learning to recommend gigs to freelancers based on their previous work and skills. So, if you've recently completed a logo design, Fiverr's AI might suggest other graphic design projects that align with your skills. The platform also recommends pricing levels based on the freelancer's experience and market trends. Freelancers using Fiverr can earn anywhere from $5 to $500 per gig, depending on the complexity of the task, making it a popular choice for skilled workers looking to make extra cash.

Content Creation: AI as Your Creative Assistant

Creating content has never been more profitable, thanks to AI tools that simplify the creative process. Content creators on platforms like **YouTube**, **Instagram**, and **TikTok** now use AI-driven tools to produce, edit, and optimize their work faster than ever.

Video Editing and Production

For example, video creators can use tools like **Descript** or **Runway** to automatically edit videos, transcribe audio, and add captions—all of which can save hours of work. **Descript**, in particular, is known for its "edit by text" feature, which lets users cut out unwanted parts of a video by simply deleting text from the transcription. This means creators can edit out mistakes or add captions in a fraction of the time it would normally take.

According to recent surveys, content creators can make anywhere from a few hundred to thousands of dollars per month, depending on their audience size and engagement. Using AI tools to streamline the production process, they can dedicate more time to growing their channels or working on sponsored content, which can significantly boost their income.

Optimizing Content for Social Media Algorithms

AI is also helping content creators understand social media algorithms, which can be notoriously difficult to predict. Tools like **VidIQ** for YouTube and **Later** for Instagram use machine learning to analyze trends, suggest optimal posting times, and identify keywords or hashtags that are currently popular. With these insights, creators can improve their chances of reaching a wider audience, leading to more views, subscribers, and, ultimately, income.

For example, **VidIQ** offers a "Scorecard" feature that shows how a video ranks for certain keywords, the best tags to use, and what your competition is doing. This helps creators refine their content strategy based on data, not guesswork. Considering that YouTube ad revenue and sponsorships can bring in significant income, especially for large channels, these AI insights can have a real impact on a creator's earnings.

Freelancing and Remote Work: AI as Your Project Manager

The world of freelancing has grown immensely, and AI is helping remote workers and freelancers find, manage, and excel in projects. Platforms like **Upwork** and **Freelancer** use AI to match freelancers with jobs, often analyzing previous work and client reviews to recommend gigs that match their skills.

Finding High-Quality Gigs Faster

For many freelancers, a significant challenge is finding quality gigs without spending hours scrolling through listings. AI-driven platforms are designed to streamline this process. For example, **Upwork** uses machine learning to match freelancers with clients who need their specific skills. As freelancers complete more jobs and build a positive reputation, Upwork's algorithm improves the types of jobs it recommends, helping them find higher-paying opportunities.

Freelancers on Upwork can earn anywhere from $10 per hour for basic tasks to over $100 per hour for specialized skills like software development. By using AI-driven matching, they can spend more time working and less time hunting for gigs, which translates to higher earnings over time.

Streamlining Administrative Tasks

Once you've landed a project, AI can also help keep you organized. Tools like **Trello** and **Notion** use AI to help freelancers manage tasks, deadlines, and communications in one place. **Trello's Butler** feature uses AI-powered automation to help freelancers create "rules" for common tasks—like moving a card to "Completed" when a due date is met or sending a reminder if a task is due in 24 hours. This minimizes administrative hassle and allows freelancers to focus on what they do best: the actual work.

AI Tools to Identify and Optimize Income Sources

Making money with AI isn't just about gig platforms and content creation; it's also about knowing how to find the best opportunities. There are several tools that leverage AI to help users identify lucrative side hustles, investment opportunities, or job options that align with their skills and goals.

Using AI to Analyze Job Markets and Trends

For those looking to make a career change or find a high-paying gig, AI-driven tools like **LinkedIn's Career Explorer**can analyze job trends and recommend roles that match a person's experience and skills. Career Explorer uses machine learning to help users understand what skills they need to land new roles, and it even suggests related job titles that may not have been on their radar.

Investing in AI-Driven Passive Income Streams

If you're looking for a more passive income approach, AI can help with that, too. Investment apps like **Betterment** and **Wealthfront** offer automated investing, where users can set financial goals, risk tolerance, and timelines, and the app's algorithm takes care of the rest. These robo-advisors use machine learning to build portfolios, rebalance them automatically, and even harvest tax losses to improve returns.

According to NerdWallet, robo-advisors can earn an average return of 5-10% per year, depending on market conditions. For users who want to grow wealth without spending hours monitoring investments, robo-advisors can be a valuable AI-driven tool for passive income.

. . .

Real-Life Examples: People Making Money with AI

Let's look at a couple of real-life examples to see how people are using AI to enhance their income:

1. **Freelance Writer Turned Content Creator**
2. Sarah, a freelance writer, decided to try content creation to diversify her income. She started a YouTube channel focused on personal finance, using tools like **Descript** to edit videos quickly and **VidIQ** to optimize her reach. After a few months, Sarah's channel gained traction, and she started earning ad revenue along with sponsorship deals. With AI-driven insights, she knew exactly when to post, what topics were trending, and how to engage her audience effectively. Today, her side income from content creation matches her earnings as a writer.
3. **Gig Worker Using AI-Powered Route Optimization**
4. Mark drives for both **Uber** and **DoorDash**. He noticed that by following Uber's AI recommendations on where to drive, he could earn more by being in high-demand areas. DoorDash's AI-driven route optimization also helped him complete more deliveries per hour. With a strategic approach and a little help from AI, Mark boosted his monthly earnings by about 30%.

Final Thoughts: Embracing the Future of Income with AI

The AI-powered income landscape is vast, flexible, and growing. Whether you're looking for a side hustle, a full-time freelancing career, or passive income opportunities, AI can help you find, manage, and optimize your earnings. The possibilities range from hands-on gigs to passive investment, making AI a powerful ally in your journey to boost your income.

With the right tools and strategies, you can take advantage of AI to earn more, save time, and focus on what matters most to you. In this new world, money-making has never been more accessible—or more tech-savvy. And as AI continues to evolve, who knows what new opportunities lie just around the corner?

Chapter 5
Investing with Robo-Advisors

Investing can be intimidating, especially if you're new to the world of stocks, bonds, and portfolios. Fortunately, there's a tool that takes much of the mystery—and some of the stress—out of investing: robo-advisors. Think of a robo-advisor as your personal financial advisor, but one who's powered by artificial intelligence and machine learning. With robo-advisors, investing is no longer a game reserved for Wall Street pros; it's something anyone can do with just a few clicks.

In this chapter, we'll break down exactly what robo-advisors are, how they work, their advantages and disadvantages, and how you can choose the best one to suit your financial goals.

What are Robo-Advisors, and How Do They Work?

A robo-advisor is an online platform that uses algorithms and data to build and manage a personalized investment portfolio on your behalf. Unlike traditional human financial advisors, robo-advisors don't require high fees or a substantial amount of money to get

started. In fact, many platforms have low (or even no) account minimums, making investing accessible for people at all financial levels.
Here's how robo-advisors work:

1. **Initial Assessment**: When you sign up for a robo-advisor, you'll typically start by answering a few questions about your financial goals, investment horizon, risk tolerance, and any specific needs you might have (like socially responsible investing preferences). Based on this assessment, the robo-advisor's algorithms will recommend a diversified investment portfolio tailored to your profile.

2. **Portfolio Construction**: Once it understands your goals and preferences, the robo-advisor will build a portfolio, usually made up of exchange-traded funds (ETFs) and, sometimes, mutual funds. ETFs are favored because they offer diversification at a low cost, tracking the performance of indexes like the S&P 500.

3. **Automated Management**: After your initial investment, the robo-advisor doesn't just leave your portfolio to sit. Instead, it actively manages it using AI algorithms. This management might include **rebalancing**, where the platform automatically adjusts the proportions of different assets in your portfolio to maintain your desired level of risk. Some robo-advisors also offer **tax-loss harvesting** (more on this in a bit), where the system strategically sells and replaces assets to minimize taxes.

4. **Ongoing Adjustments and Recommendations**: Robo-advisors monitor market trends, analyze economic factors, and adjust your portfolio as needed. The goal is to keep your investments aligned with your objectives, regardless of what the market is doing.

Popular robo-advisors include **Betterment**, **Wealthfront**, **Ellevest**, and **Fidelity Go**. Each platform offers unique features, but the general process is largely similar across services.

Pros of Using Robo-Advisors

Robo-advisors have become popular for a reason. Here are some of the biggest advantages they offer:

1. Low Fees and Account Minimums

Traditional financial advisors often charge high fees, sometimes around 1% or more of your total assets under management. Robo-advisors, on the other hand, charge significantly lower fees—usually between 0.25% and 0.5% annually. This lower fee structure makes investing more accessible and allows you to keep more of your returns.

Account minimums are also generally low. For example, Betterment has no minimum, Wealthfront has a $500 minimum, and Ellevest requires only $1. These low entry barriers make robo-advisors a viable option for beginner investors or those without a large amount to invest initially.

2. Automated Rebalancing

One of the biggest challenges for individual investors is maintaining the right asset allocation over time. As market values fluctuate, your portfolio's allocation may drift away from its target (say, from 60% stocks and 40% bonds to 70% stocks and 30% bonds). Rebalancing manually is not only time-consuming but can also be costly in terms of transaction fees and tax implications.

Robo-advisors automate this process, rebalancing portfolios regularly to maintain the investor's desired risk level. For example, Wealthfront's algorithms continuously monitor and rebalance client portfolios to keep them aligned with risk tolerance.

3. Tax-Loss Harvesting

Tax-loss harvesting is a strategy that can help investors offset gains by selling securities at a loss and replacing them with similar investments. Many robo-advisors, including Betterment and Wealth-front, offer this feature as a standard service for taxable accounts. According to Betterment, tax-loss harvesting can increase returns by as much as 0.77% per year, which can compound significantly over time.

4. Accessibility and Ease of Use

Robo-advisors offer an accessible, user-friendly experience. Most platforms provide detailed dashboards where investors can view their portfolio's performance, understand their asset allocation, and make adjustments as needed. These interfaces are designed to make complex financial data digestible, with simple graphs, projections, and explanations that help beginners understand their investments.

5. Goal-Based Investing

Robo-advisors often focus on goal-based investing, meaning they structure your portfolio around your specific objectives, such as retirement, buying a house, or saving for a child's education. This is a huge advantage for people who have clear financial goals but aren't sure how to align their investments with these objectives.

Cons of Using Robo-Advisors

While robo-advisors offer many advantages, they aren't for everyone. Here are a few of the downsides to consider:

1. Limited Personalization

While robo-advisors do customize portfolios based on your risk tolerance and goals, the level of personalization is still limited compared to what a human advisor can offer. If you have complex financial needs—such as estate planning, tax optimization across multiple accounts, or strategies involving private assets—a robo-advisor might not be able to handle everything effectively.

2. Less Human Interaction

For investors who appreciate personalized advice, a robo-advisor might feel too impersonal. While some platforms like Betterment offer hybrid models with access to human advisors for an additional fee, the guidance is generally limited to basic financial planning and may lack the in-depth analysis a dedicated financial advisor could provide.

3. Not Ideal for Short-Term Goals

Robo-advisors are designed for long-term investing. If you need access to your funds in the near term, such as within a year or two, robo-advisors may not be the best choice. Their portfolios are typically designed for growth over time, and short-term withdrawals could mean facing losses if the market is down.

4. Lack of Control

Robo-advisors manage your portfolio with little input from you, which can be a downside for investors who prefer a hands-on approach. The algorithms determine asset allocation, buying, and selling decisions, meaning you have limited control over the specific assets you hold. If you enjoy managing your own portfolio and researching individual stocks, a robo-advisor may feel restrictive.

Choosing the Best Robo-Advisor for Your Goals and Risk Tolerance

Choosing the right robo-advisor depends on your financial goals, risk tolerance, and personal preferences. Here's a guide to help you find the best option for your needs:

1. Identify Your Investment Goals

Are you saving for retirement, a home, or your child's education? Different robo-advisors cater to different goals. Betterment and Wealthfront, for example, offer goal-based investing tools and can customize portfolios for various timelines and financial targets.

For women-specific investing needs, **Ellevest** has tailored portfolios and financial education tools geared toward helping women overcome the gender wealth gap.

2. Consider Your Risk Tolerance

When choosing a robo-advisor, it's essential to understand your risk tolerance—how much volatility you're willing to endure. Most robo-advisors ask questions about your comfort with risk and use that data to recommend a portfolio that fits your tolerance. **Fidelity Go** offers conservative, moderate, and aggressive portfolio options to match different risk levels.

3. Evaluate the Fees and Minimum Requirements

Some robo-advisors, like Betterment and Wealthfront, charge a management fee of around 0.25% per year. Others, like SoFi Invest, offer no management fees, though they may have more limited features. Compare the fee structure and minimum requirements to ensure they align with your budget.

4. Look at Additional Features

If you're interested in extra features like tax-loss harvesting, human advisor access, or socially responsible investing (SRI), make sure the robo-advisor you choose offers these options. For example, Betterment offers an SRI portfolio, while Wealthfront and Schwab Intelligent Portfolios include tax-loss harvesting as standard.

5. User Experience and Interface

Robo-advisors are designed to be user-friendly, but some platforms are more intuitive than others. Most offer a demo or trial period, so try a few out to see which one feels most comfortable. Betterment, for instance, is known for its clear interface, while Wealthfront's detailed goal-based dashboard provides in-depth financial planning tools.

Real-Life Example: Choosing the Right Robo-Advisor

Consider Sarah, a young professional who wants to start investing but has limited time and funds. She's saving for retirement and wants a low-cost, hands-off investment option with tax advantages. After researching her options, Sarah chooses **Wealthfront** for its goal-based planning tools, low fees (0.25% annually), and tax-loss harvesting. She starts with the minimum investment of $500, knowing that Wealthfront will automatically manage her portfolio and keep her on track for her retirement goal.

. . .

Final Thoughts: Are Robo-Advisors Right for You?

Robo-advisors have transformed investing from something complex and intimidating into a process that's accessible to almost anyone. With low fees, automated management, and options for beginners, robo-advisors make it easier than ever to start building wealth.

However, it's essential to remember that robo-advisors aren't a one-size-fits-all solution. They're best suited for those with long-term goals and a preference for hands-off investing. If you're someone who wants more control over your investments, or if you need highly personalized financial planning, a traditional financial advisor might still be the better choice.

In the end, robo-advisors offer a valuable tool for those looking to invest with minimal effort and maximum efficiency. By understanding their pros and cons and choosing the right platform for your needs, you can use robo-advisors to grow your wealth and achieve your financial goals with the power of AI at your side.

Chapter 6
Decentralized Finance (DeFi) and Cryptocurrency Investment

Cryptocurrency and decentralized finance (DeFi) are reshaping the financial landscape by giving people more control over their money without needing traditional banks. As we dive into this chapter, we'll cover the basics of DeFi, explore digital assets like cryptocurrency and NFTs, and examine both the potential rewards and significant risks involved in this rapidly evolving field.

What is Decentralized Finance (DeFi), and How Could It Disrupt Traditional Finance?

Decentralized finance, or DeFi, refers to a network of financial services built on blockchain technology—typically the Ethereum blockchain—that operates without centralized intermediaries like banks or brokerages. Instead of relying on traditional institutions, DeFi uses **smart contracts**—self-executing code on the blockchain—to automate financial transactions. This system enables borrowing, lending, trading, and earning interest in a completely decentralized way.

. . .

How DeFi Works

The DeFi ecosystem relies on blockchain, a digital ledger that records all transactions securely and transparently. Key components of DeFi include:

1. **Smart Contracts**: These are pieces of code that automatically execute transactions when specific conditions are met. For instance, if you take out a loan on a DeFi platform, a smart contract will enforce repayment terms without needing a human intermediary.
2. **Decentralized Apps (DApps)**: These applications operate on a blockchain and provide services similar to traditional banks, such as loans, savings accounts, and even insurance. Platforms like **Aave** and **Compound** allow users to lend and borrow assets, while **Uniswap** and **SushiSwap** enable decentralized trading.
3. **Stablecoins**: Since many cryptocurrencies fluctuate in value, stablecoins—digital assets pegged to stable assets like the U.S. dollar—help stabilize transactions in the DeFi space. Examples include **USDC** and **DAI**.

By eliminating the need for banks and financial intermediaries, DeFi offers lower fees, faster transaction speeds, and greater accessibility. According to a report by DeFi Pulse, as of late 2022, billions of dollars are "locked" in DeFi protocols, indicating the massive interest and capital in this space.

Potential to Disrupt Traditional Finance

DeFi's potential lies in its ability to democratize finance. Traditional banking services require credit checks, have high fees, and are accessible mainly to those with existing wealth. DeFi, on the other hand, allows anyone with an internet connection to participate in financial activities, often with lower fees and more transparency.

1. **Borrowing and Lending**: DeFi platforms let users borrow and lend without needing a bank, with interest rates often higher for lenders than traditional banks. In 2022, the average DeFi lending interest rate was around 7%, significantly higher than most savings accounts in traditional finance.
2. **Investment Opportunities**: DeFi opens up new possibilities for earning returns, including liquidity mining (providing assets to a DeFi platform to facilitate transactions) and yield farming (moving assets across platforms to maximize returns). These innovative options don't exist in traditional finance.
3. **Financial Inclusion**: DeFi has the potential to provide banking services to millions of "unbanked" people worldwide. This system requires no credit history, and it's open to anyone with an internet connection and a cryptocurrency wallet.

Despite its potential, DeFi is still in its early stages, and the space is risky and volatile. The lack of regulation, potential for hacking, and market instability make it a high-stakes arena.

An Introduction to Cryptocurrency, NFTs, and Digital Assets

Cryptocurrency is the foundation of the DeFi world. These digital assets rely on blockchain technology to create a decentralized, secure way to store and transfer value. Let's break down some of the key types of digital assets:

1. Cryptocurrency

Cryptocurrencies are digital or virtual currencies that rely on cryptography for security and decentralized networks to verify transactions. The most popular cryptocurrencies include **Bitcoin** (BTC), **Ethereum** (ETH), and **Solana** (SOL). While Bitcoin primarily serves as a store of value or "digital gold," Ethereum, Solana, and other altcoins are designed to support DeFi applications and smart contracts.

As of late 2023, the market for cryptocurrency continues to grow, with Bitcoin leading in value and Ethereum driving the development of DeFi through its smart contract capabilities.

2. Non-Fungible Tokens (NFTs)

NFTs are unique digital assets that represent ownership of a specific item, such as digital art, music, or even virtual real estate. Unlike cryptocurrencies, which are fungible (one Bitcoin is the same as another), NFTs are unique, and each token has individual value. The NFT market exploded in 2021, with artists and creators selling digital art, collectibles, and other items directly to buyers.

Popular NFT marketplaces include **OpenSea** and **Rarible**, where users can buy, sell, and trade NFTs. However, the NFT market is highly speculative, with prices often swinging wildly based on trends, social media buzz, and celebrity endorsements. NFTs' value lies not just in their investment potential but in their ability to provide creators with new ways to monetize their work.

3. Stablecoins

As mentioned earlier, stablecoins are a type of cryptocurrency pegged to stable assets like the U.S. dollar or gold, providing a more stable value. **Tether (USDT)** and **USD Coin (USDC)** are examples. Stablecoins play a critical role in DeFi by allowing users to engage in transactions without worrying about the volatility of traditional cryptocurrencies.

Risks and Rewards: Navigating This High-Stakes Investment Area

DeFi and cryptocurrencies offer exciting opportunities, but they also come with significant risks. Understanding both sides is crucial before diving in.

The Rewards of DeFi and Cryptocurrency Investment

1. **High Potential Returns**: The DeFi space is known for its high return potential. For instance, yield farming and liquidity mining can generate double-digit or even triple-digit annual percentage yields (APY) on certain platforms. However, these returns come with high risks and often fluctuate drastically.

2. **Decentralized Control**: DeFi allows users to control their finances directly, bypassing traditional banking. With DeFi, individuals retain custody of their assets through personal wallets, without depending on banks or intermediaries.

3. **Innovation and Access**: DeFi and cryptocurrency bring new financial opportunities to underserved communities and the unbanked. With DeFi protocols and cryptocurrencies, anyone with an internet connection can participate in the global financial system, offering greater accessibility.

The Risks of DeFi and Cryptocurrency Investment

1. **Volatility**: Cryptocurrencies are notoriously volatile. Bitcoin's price, for example, dropped from nearly $65,000 in November 2021 to below $20,000 in 2022, highlighting how quickly the market can change. Volatility presents a substantial risk for investors, especially those who may need quick access to their funds.

2. **Regulatory Uncertainty**: The regulatory landscape for DeFi and cryptocurrencies is still developing. Governments are considering regulations that could impact DeFi platforms, potentially affecting their operation and, in some cases, user access. Countries like China have already banned cryptocurrency trading, while others, like the U.S., are tightening regulations.

3. **Security Risks and Scams**: While blockchain itself is secure, DeFi platforms are vulnerable to hacks and scams. According to data from CipherTrace, DeFi-related hacks and fraud accounted for $1.9 billion in losses in 2021 alone. Many platforms have limited protections, making users responsible for their own security.

4. **Smart Contract Risks**: Since DeFi transactions are based on smart contracts, flaws in the code can lead to losses. For example, in 2020, the **DeFi protocol bZx** was hacked twice in one week, leading to a loss of nearly $1 million due to vulnerabilities in its smart contracts. Errors in smart contract code can expose users to significant financial risk.

5. **Complexity and Knowledge Requirements**: DeFi isn't as straightforward as traditional finance, and understanding how to navigate DeFi protocols, smart contracts, and various wallets can be daunting. For new investors, the learning curve can lead to costly mistakes if they don't fully understand the risks involved.

Tips for Navigating DeFi and Cryptocurrency Investments

If you're interested in DeFi and cryptocurrency but want to manage the risks, here are some strategies to consider:

1. **Start Small and Diversify**: Start with a small investment, especially if you're new to DeFi and

cryptocurrency. Diversify across different digital assets rather than putting everything into one coin or platform. Diversification can help mitigate losses if one asset underperforms.

2. **Do Your Research**: Not all DeFi platforms and cryptocurrencies are created equal. Thoroughly research any platform you plan to use and check its security history. Look for established DeFi protocols like Aave, Compound, and Uniswap, which have been around longer and have more robust security measures.

3. **Use Reputable Wallets and Keep Your Keys Secure**: If you're investing in DeFi, you'll need a secure digital wallet. Hardware wallets like **Ledger** and **Trezor** are popular for storing large amounts of cryptocurrency safely offline. Always keep your private keys secure; if someone else gains access, they can transfer your assets.

4. **Stay Informed on Regulatory Changes**: Regulatory developments can impact DeFi platforms and cryptocurrency values, so staying updated on global regulations is essential. The U.S. Securities and Exchange Commission (SEC), for example, is increasingly involved in regulating crypto assets, and these changes can directly affect your investments.

5. **Be Cautious with High-Yield Opportunities**: While high yields in DeFi can be tempting, they also come with high risks. Avoid "too good to be true" offers and understand the potential for losses. In general, stablecoin lending provides lower but more reliable yields compared to speculative DeFi protocols.

6. **Understand Tax Implications**: Many countries, including the U.S., treat cryptocurrency gains as taxable events. Be aware of how taxes apply to your investments, as even small transactions may need to be reported.

. . .

Final Thoughts: Is DeFi and Cryptocurrency Right for You?

Investing in DeFi and cryptocurrency can be a double-edged sword: it offers exciting potential returns but requires thorough knowledge, careful risk management, and a stomach for volatility. While these digital assets and platforms bring new opportunities for building wealth, they also come with risks that traditional investments don't carry.

For risk-tolerant investors who are willing to stay informed and prioritize security, DeFi and cryptocurrency offer a path to financial independence beyond traditional banking. However, the key to success lies in understanding the tools, platforms, and potential pitfalls in this complex but promising area of finance. With thoughtful research and a balanced approach, DeFi and cryptocurrency can be a valuable addition to your portfolio, opening the door to the future of finance.

Part Three

Saving Money Efficiently with AI

Chapter 7
AI-Driven Budgeting and Expense Tracking

Reminder: If budgeting was identified as a priority in your DIY Financial Health Check, this chapter will introduce AI-powered tools and strategies to help you set up, track, and optimize your budget. Whether you're new to budgeting or looking for ways to improve, the tools here will be a great fit for your needs.

In a world where everything seems to be getting more expensive, budgeting effectively can be a serious challenge. But thanks to artificial intelligence (AI), managing money and setting financial goals has become easier and more efficient. AI-powered budgeting apps and tools have transformed how we track spending, save, and make decisions about our finances. In this chapter, we'll explore popular AI-driven budgeting apps, how they automate saving, track spending, and offer practical tips on using these tools to set and achieve your financial goals.

. . .

Overview of Popular AI-Powered Budgeting Apps and Tools

AI-powered budgeting apps don't just track your expenses; they analyze your financial habits, predict future spending, and even offer personalized advice to help you reach your goals. Here's a look at some of the most popular options available today.

1. Mint

Mint, developed by Intuit, is one of the most widely used budgeting apps, and it uses AI to categorize transactions, track spending patterns, and offer insights on where you might be over-spending. Mint integrates with your bank accounts, credit cards, and even investment accounts, giving you a comprehensive picture of your finances in one place.

Features:

- Expense categorization and transaction tracking
- Bill tracking and reminders
- Personalized spending insights
- Goal-setting for saving and debt reduction

AI-Driven Benefits: Mint's AI automatically categorizes your spending, alerts you when you're approaching your budget limits, and identifies spending trends. For example, it might notify you that you're spending more on dining out than usual or remind you of upcoming bills to avoid late fees.

2. You Need a Budget (YNAB)

YNAB is a popular budgeting app that encourages users to assign every dollar a job. It's based on a proactive budgeting philosophy, and its AI-driven features make it easy to stay on track. YNAB's AI learns your spending habits over time and helps you create a realistic monthly budget.

Features:

- Goal tracking for savings and debt payoff
- Real-time expense tracking and reporting
- Personalized recommendations based on spending patterns

AI-Driven Benefits: YNAB's AI analyzes your spending history and provides recommendations to help you save more each month. For example, if it notices that you tend to overspend on groceries, it might suggest creating a specific budget category for that, helping you stay within limits.

3. PocketGuard

PocketGuard is an app that focuses on helping users stay within their spending limits by showing exactly how much money is "safe to spend." PocketGuard's AI algorithms analyze your bills, savings goals, and spending patterns to determine what's left after covering essentials.

Features:

- Real-time view of "safe-to-spend" money
- Automated savings goals
- Bill tracking and subscription management

AI-Driven Benefits: PocketGuard's AI calculates a safe-to-spend amount based on your budget, recurring bills, and savings goals. It provides a clear picture of your daily financial flexibility, which can be particularly helpful for those who need help avoiding over-spending.

4. Empower (formerly Personal Capital)

Empower combines AI-driven budgeting with investment tracking, making it ideal for users who want to manage their cash flow while keeping an eye on long-term wealth building. Empower's AI-based analytics provide insights on spending, saving, and investing habits.

Features:

- Budgeting and cash flow analysis
- Retirement and investment tracking
- Personalized advice on savings and investment strategies

AI-Driven Benefits: Empower's AI analyzes your spending and provides advice on managing cash flow and investing. It also offers retirement planning tools that use your current spending to project future needs, helping you stay on track with long-term goals.

5. Qapital

Qapital is a savings-focused app that uses "rules" to automate your savings based on triggers. For example, every time you buy coffee, Qapital can set aside $1 for your vacation fund. This rule-based approach leverages AI to help you save without thinking about it actively.

Features:

- Savings goals and rules-based automation
- Round-up savings
- Financial goal tracking and progress monitoring

AI-Driven Benefits: Qapital's AI allows you to create customized savings rules based on your habits. This automates savings based on your daily activities, helping you build savings effortlessly. The app also provides feedback on your progress toward financial goals.

. . .

Automating Savings with AI and Tracking Spending Patterns

One of the biggest advantages of AI-driven budgeting apps is their ability to automate savings and track spending patterns without requiring you to constantly update a spreadsheet. Here's how these apps help automate your finances.

1. Automated Savings

Many AI-powered budgeting apps now offer automatic savings features, where the app moves small amounts of money into a savings account based on rules or predictions. For instance, **Digit** is an AI-driven app that analyzes your income and spending patterns to determine how much you can afford to save. It then moves small amounts of money into a savings account periodically, without you even noticing it.

Example: Digit might notice that you've been spending less on transportation this month (perhaps due to working from home), and it could increase your automated savings accordingly. By moving small amounts that you won't miss, these apps can help you build up savings over time.

2. Tracking Spending Patterns

AI-driven budgeting apps categorize your spending automatically and show you where your money is going. Over time, the AI learns your habits and offers insights that can help you make adjustments.

Example: If you've been spending more on dining out than usual, Mint might alert you and suggest reducing your dining budget. This is valuable for users who may not realize where small expenses add up over time.

3. Predictive Budgeting

Some budgeting tools, like PocketGuard, offer predictive budgeting features. These apps analyze your income, recurring bills, and typical spending patterns to estimate your future expenses. Predictive budgeting helps you avoid cash flow problems and ensures that you're setting aside enough money to cover bills and other essentials.

Example: PocketGuard's AI may notice that your rent and utility bills are due in a few days, and it will adjust your "safe-to-spend" amount to account for these upcoming expenses, helping you avoid overspending.

Tips on Using AI Tools to Set Realistic Financial Goals and Stay Accountable

AI-powered budgeting tools can be incredibly effective in helping you set achievable financial goals and stay on track. Here are some tips for maximizing their potential:

1. Set Clear, Achievable Goals

The first step in using AI-driven budgeting tools effectively is to define specific financial goals. Whether it's saving for a vacation, paying off debt, or building an emergency fund, having a clear target helps the AI provide better recommendations.

Example: If your goal is to build an emergency fund of $1,000, you can set this target in an app like Qapital. The app's AI will then use your chosen rules (such as rounding up each purchase) to gradually move money into your savings, helping you reach that goal over time.

2. Customize Spending Categories

Most AI budgeting apps allow you to customize spending categories, which makes tracking more accurate and relevant to your needs. For example, if you have specific categories like "pet care" or "coffee" that don't fit into standard categories, creating these can help you see exactly where your money is going.

Example: Mint allows users to create custom categories, and its AI will automatically track your spending in these categories, making it easier to adjust and set realistic budgets based on your actual lifestyle.

3. Regularly Review Spending Insights

One of the most powerful aspects of AI budgeting apps is their ability to provide insights into your spending habits. Make it a habit to review these insights regularly—once a week or once a month. This can help you spot any trends, like overspending on non-essential items, and make adjustments.

Example: Every month, Empower provides a "Spending Overview" report that shows where your money went. Reviewing this report can help you identify areas where you might want to cut back or where you could allocate more funds to savings or debt repayment.

4. Set Up Notifications and Alerts

Most AI-powered budgeting apps offer notifications and alerts to help you stay on track. These might include alerts for upcoming bills, budget limit warnings, or reminders to check your progress toward savings goals. Setting up these alerts can keep you accountable without requiring you to check the app constantly.

Example: PocketGuard allows users to set alerts for when they approach their spending limits in certain categories. If you're nearing the limit on your dining budget, you'll get a notification—prompting you to either adjust your spending or reduce costs in other areas.

5. Use Savings Automation for Small Wins

Automated savings rules, like those offered by Qapital, can help you save effortlessly. Set up small, automated transfers tied to your daily habits, like saving $1 every time you order coffee. Over time, these micro-savings add up, helping you reach your financial goals faster.

Example: Using Qapital's "Round-Up" rule, every purchase is rounded up to the nearest dollar, and the difference is saved. If you spend $3.60 on coffee, $0.40 goes into savings. Over time, these small amounts can accumulate into a larger savings fund with minimal effort on your part.

. . .

Final Thoughts: Using AI to Simplify and Strengthen Your Budgeting

AI-driven budgeting tools offer a powerful way to manage your finances with minimal effort. By automating savings, tracking spending patterns, and providing personalized insights, these tools make it easier to stick to a budget and reach your financial goals.

With a variety of apps available, each with unique features and AI capabilities, there's a budgeting tool for every lifestyle

Case Study: Renee's Financial Transformation

Case Study: Renee's Financial Transformation

Renee, a 27-year-old from Sydney, leveraged AI-driven budgeting tools to enhance her financial management. Initially exploring AI for general purposes, she transitioned to using it for budgeting upon friends' recommendations. The AI provided personalized suggestions for budgeting strategies and investment opportunities, enabling her to save $5,000 and gain a better understanding of financial concepts without sifting through conflicting advice.

Quick Start Guide to Budgeting with AI

Quick Start Guide to Budgeting with AI

1. **Download a Budgeting App**
2. Choose a reputable AI-driven budgeting app like Mint, You Need a Budget (YNAB), or PocketGuard.
3. **Connect Your Bank Accounts**
4. Safely connect your bank accounts to the app to allow for automatic tracking and categorization of your expenses.
5. **Set Up Categories and Spending Limits**
6. Use the app's AI recommendations or create your own categories, such as groceries, dining, and utilities. Set realistic limits based on your spending patterns.
7. **Review Spending Patterns**
8. After a week, check the app's insights. Look for any trends or areas where you're overspending.
9. **Set a Financial Goal**
10. Use the app's goal-setting feature to create a specific savings target, like building an emergency fund or saving for a vacation.

Chapter 8
Smarter Shopping with AI

Reminder: **If you found that saving and managing your expenses could use some extra support, this chapter will guide you through AI-powered tools designed to find deals, manage subscriptions, and build savings. Your Health Check is a great starting point to personalize the approaches covered here.**

Shopping has evolved dramatically in the last decade, with artificial intelligence now offering smart solutions for everything from finding the best deals to personalizing discounts. AI-powered tools can transform how we shop, helping us save time and money by finding the best prices, applying discounts, and even providing personalized recommendations. In this chapter, we'll look at how AI is revolutionizing shopping with price comparison tools, deal-finding apps, personalized discounts, and the future of digital coupons.

. . .

Using AI-Powered Price Comparison Tools and Deal-Finding Apps

AI-powered price comparison tools are a game-changer for budget-conscious shoppers. Gone are the days of manually checking prices across multiple websites; these tools do the legwork for you, scanning various retailers to ensure you're getting the best deal.

1. Google Shopping

Google Shopping uses AI to compare prices across multiple online retailers. When you search for a product, Google's algorithms scan prices from different sellers, showing you options that include shipping costs and estimated delivery times. By aggregating data from countless retailers, Google Shopping saves you time and ensures that you find the most competitive price.

2. Honey

Honey, a popular browser extension owned by PayPal, automatically finds and applies the best available coupons at checkout for many online retailers. Its AI scans and tests promo codes, applying them to your cart if they're valid. Honey also has a price comparison tool that shows you price history data, so you know if a discount is genuine or just marketing hype.

Example: Honey's "Droplist" feature allows users to track the price of specific items. If the price drops, Honey sends an alert, helping you buy at the optimal moment. Honey's price history and alert features have saved users an average of $126 per year, according to PayPal's research on Honey's impact.

3. CamelCamelCamel

For Amazon shoppers, **CamelCamelCamel** is a dedicated price tracking tool that monitors prices on Amazon and notifies users of price drops. This tool helps avoid impulse purchases by alerting you when an item you're interested in reaches your target price. CamelCamelCamel's AI-powered tracking helps users make informed buying decisions by showing historical price trends, revealing whether an item is truly on sale or just cycling through Amazon's dynamic pricing.

4. ShopSavvy

ShopSavvy is an app that lets users scan barcodes in stores and compare prices with online and local retailers. ShopSavvy's AI aggregates price data from both online and in-store sources, ensuring users get the best possible deal wherever they are. It also has price-drop alerts and coupons for additional savings.

Example: ShopSavvy's in-store scanning feature is particularly useful for comparing prices at nearby stores. If a store offers price matching, you can show the app's price comparison to get a discount instantly.

How AI Personalizes Discounts, Rewards, and Cashback Offers

AI not only helps you find the best prices but also offers personalized discounts, rewards, and cashback options. These features are often tailored based on your shopping habits, preferences, and purchasing history. Here's a closer look at how AI is making rewards and discounts more relevant to individual shoppers.

1. Personalized Discounts through Retail Apps

Retailers like **Target** and **Walmart** use AI to tailor discounts and recommendations to each customer. Target's app, for example, offers personalized deals and promotions through its Target Circle rewards program. The app's AI analyzes past purchases and browsing history, providing personalized offers that encourage customers to return to the store.

Example: Target Circle might offer a discount on items you've purchased frequently, such as 10% off your favorite brand of coffee. This personalization not only enhances the shopping experience but also builds customer loyalty.

2. AI-Driven Cashback Offers with Rakuten

Rakuten (formerly Ebates) is a cashback app and browser extension that partners with thousands of retailers to provide cashback on purchases. Rakuten uses AI to recommend cashback offers that align with your shopping habits. For example, if you frequently shop for electronics, Rakuten may prioritize cashback deals from electronic retailers in your account.

Rakuten's AI also sends alerts when cashback rates increase for certain stores, ensuring that users don't miss out on higher rewards. According to Rakuten, users can earn an average of $10 to $25 per month in cashback, depending on their spending habits and the stores they frequent.

3. Card-Linked Offers with Dosh

Dosh is a cashback app that links directly to your debit or credit card and automatically applies cashback offers when you make a purchase at participating retailers. Unlike traditional reward programs, you don't have to clip coupons or apply codes; Dosh's AI detects eligible transactions and credits cashback to your account automatically.

Example: Dosh partners with retailers like Walmart, Sephora, and Dunkin', offering anywhere from 2% to 10% cashback on purchases. For users who frequently shop at these stores, cashback adds up quickly, making it an easy way to save without any extra effort.

The Future of Digital Coupons and Tailored Shopping Experiences

Digital coupons and tailored shopping experiences are advancing rapidly, with AI enabling more personalized and context-aware savings. Traditional paper coupons are increasingly giving way to digital offers that are targeted, dynamic, and customized in real-time.

1. Dynamic Digital Coupons

Unlike static paper coupons, digital coupons can change based on various factors, such as location, purchase history, or even time of day. Retailers like **Kroger** and **Safeway** are using AI to offer dynamic discounts to customers, tailored to each shopper's unique profile.

For instance, Kroger's app provides personalized discounts on products you frequently purchase. It even offers customized weekly deals based on your shopping habits, ensuring you get relevant discounts each time you visit the store.

Example: Kroger's AI-driven platform might notice that you frequently buy organic produce. It could then offer you a personalized 15% discount on organic vegetables for a limited time, making your shopping experience more relevant and cost-effective.

2. Location-Based Discounts

Retailers are also leveraging AI to deliver location-based discounts through mobile apps. For example, **Starbucks** uses geolocation to send customers promotions when they're near a store, encouraging them to stop in and make a purchase. This type of contextual promotion leverages AI to make deals more timely and relevant.

Example: If you walk past a Starbucks, the app might send you an offer for $2 off your favorite drink, encouraging you to stop in. These location-based deals not only increase customer engagement but also provide immediate, targeted savings.

3. Voice-Activated Shopping and AI-Powered Assistance

Voice-activated devices like **Amazon Alexa** and **Google Assistant** are changing how people shop, making it as simple as saying, "Alexa, find me the best deal on coffee." These smart assistants use AI to search for deals, compare prices, and even apply discounts where possible. Amazon's Alexa, for instance, can notify users of discounts on frequently purchased items and suggest lower-cost alternatives.

AI-powered voice assistants are expected to play a significant role in the future of shopping, helping consumers find deals effortlessly and make informed purchasing decisions without having to browse manually.

4. Augmented Reality (AR) and AI in Shopping

Some retailers are using augmented reality (AR) combined with AI to enhance the shopping experience. For example, **IKEA's Place**

app allows users to visualize furniture in their homes before buying, which can prevent costly mistakes. Sephora's Virtual Artist tool uses AR and AI to let users "try on" makeup virtually, giving them a better sense of whether a product is a good fit.

This fusion of AR and AI is expected to grow, enabling shoppers to make more informed decisions and avoid returns, ultimately saving money in the long run.

Tips for Using AI Tools to Maximize Savings and Enhance Your Shopping Experience

Here are some tips on making the most of AI-driven shopping tools and features:

1. **Use Multiple Apps for Comprehensive Savings**: Install several AI-driven tools like Honey, Rakuten, and Dosh to ensure you're capturing savings in multiple forms (e.g., coupons, cashback, price tracking). Each tool offers a unique set of benefits, so using them together can maximize your overall savings.

2. **Set Price Alerts and Track Price History**: Use apps like CamelCamelCamel or Honey's Droplist feature to track price history and set alerts. Knowing an item's price history can help you determine if a sale is genuinely a good deal or just a temporary markdown.

3. **Link Your Credit Cards for Automatic Cashback**: Apps like Dosh and Rakuten link directly to your credit or debit card, automatically applying cashback deals without needing to take extra steps. This can be especially useful if you're prone to forgetting to use cashback offers.

4. **Personalize Your Experience by Allowing Data Access**: Some apps personalize discounts and recommendations based on your shopping habits, which

requires permission to access your data. By allowing apps like Target or Kroger access to your purchase history, you can receive more relevant discounts, though it's essential to review privacy policies and ensure you're comfortable with the data-sharing aspects.

5. **Stay Organized with a Budgeting App**: To make sure your savings don't lead to overspending, consider using an AI-powered budgeting app like Mint or YNAB alongside your shopping tools. Budgeting apps track your spending and help you stay within your budget while taking advantage of AI-powered deals and discounts.

Final Thoughts: The Future of AI-Driven Shopping

AI-driven shopping tools have already transformed how we buy and save, making the process smarter, faster, and more tailored to our needs. As these technologies continue to advance, we can expect even more personalized discounts, dynamic pricing adjustments, and seamless integration with everyday shopping experiences.

With AI-powered tools, finding the best price, getting personalized deals, and even receiving discounts as you approach a store have become easy and accessible to anyone with a smartphone. By adopting these AI tools, you're not only saving money but also enhancing the shopping experience, turning what used to be a tedious process into a more enjoyable—and rewarding—activity.

Quick Start Guide to Saving on Everyday Purchases

Quick Start Guide to Saving on Everyday Purchases

1. **Install a Deal-Finding Browser Extension**
2. Try a tool like Honey or Rakuten to automatically find and apply coupons when shopping online.
3. **Set Up Price Alerts**
4. Use apps like CamelCamelCamel or Honey's Droplist to track prices on items you want. Get notified when prices drop to avoid impulse buying.
5. **Manage Subscriptions**
6. Use an app like Rocket Money (Truebill) to identify recurring subscriptions. Review and cancel any that you're not actively using.
7. **Automate Small Savings**
8. Set up a rule-based savings app like Qapital, which can save small amounts each time you make a purchase or round up your change to the nearest dollar.
9. **Check for Personalized Cashback Offers**

10. Link your cards to cashback apps like Dosh or Rakuten to earn money back on everyday purchases.

Chapter 9
Optimizing Bills and Reducing Debt with AI

Reminder: If debt management and bill tracking emerged as focus areas in your Health Check, this chapter will be especially relevant. Here, you'll learn about AI tools that can negotiate bills, monitor payments, and create a structured plan to pay down debt.

Managing bills and tackling debt can be overwhelming, but AI-powered tools are making it easier to take control of these aspects of personal finance. From negotiating lower bills to automating debt payments, AI is providing new ways to save money and pay down debt more efficiently. In this chapter, we'll explore AI-powered bill negotiation tools, subscription management apps, debt analysis features, and services that automate payments and interest tracking, all of which can help you reduce financial stress and achieve your goals.

. . .

AI-Powered Bill Negotiation Tools and Subscription Management

One of the fastest ways to reduce monthly expenses is by lowering recurring bills and managing unnecessary subscriptions. AI-powered tools have emerged to negotiate bills on your behalf and track active subscriptions, which can quickly lead to significant savings.

1. Trim

Trim is an AI-driven app that specializes in bill negotiation and subscription management. Once you connect your accounts, Trim's algorithms analyze your recurring bills and subscriptions, looking for areas where it can save you money. Trim negotiates bills like cable, internet, and phone services by contacting your providers directly and requesting discounts or reductions. Trim charges a fee of 33% of the savings it achieves, but only if it successfully reduces your bill.

Example: If Trim manages to negotiate a $100 reduction on your internet bill, it would take a one-time $33 fee, saving you the remaining $67. According to Trim, users save an average of $620 per year, though actual savings depend on individual bills and service providers.

Trim also helps with subscription management by identifying recurring payments and alerting you to subscriptions you might want to cancel. This feature is especially useful for people who tend to forget about trial subscriptions or minor services that add up over time.

2. Truebill (now Rocket Money)

Rocket Money, formerly known as Truebill, offers a similar range of services, focusing on bill negotiation and subscription management. Its AI scans your accounts for recurring charges, identifies bills with potential savings, and handles the negotiation process for you. Rocket Money charges a success fee between 30% and 60% of the savings, which varies depending on the provider and bill type.

Rocket Money also tracks and categorizes subscriptions, allowing you to see everything you're paying for in one dashboard.

You can even cancel subscriptions directly through the app, making it easy to cut costs without the hassle of calling individual companies.

Example: Rocket Money's data shows that many users have saved hundreds of dollars annually by canceling unused subscriptions. It also provides users with bill reminders, so they avoid late fees, another common financial pitfall.

3. Billshark

Billshark is another AI-powered negotiation service that targets cable, internet, and phone bills, as well as subscription services. Billshark's team uses AI-assisted negotiation techniques to lower your bills by negotiating directly with service providers. Similar to Trim and Rocket Money, Billshark charges a percentage of the savings they achieve (typically 40%).

Example: A 2021 report by Billshark showed that its average customer saved about $300 per year. The service is particularly effective for people with high utility or internet bills, as these often have room for negotiation.

4. Hiatus

Hiatus uses AI to monitor your bills and look for ways to reduce them. It also helps identify hidden fees and provides bill negotiation support. Hiatus has a proactive approach: if it detects a higher-than-usual charge on a bill, it can flag it for review, potentially helping you save money on unexpected price hikes.

Hiatus, like the other services, charges a success fee if it manages to lower your bills. Its subscription management feature also keeps track of all your monthly expenses, helping you see a clear picture of where your money is going.

How AI Can Help You Analyze and Lower Your Debt

Debt is a common financial burden, and AI-powered tools are now available to help you manage, analyze, and reduce it. By using algorithms to evaluate your financial situation and suggest customized debt reduction plans, AI-driven apps can guide you toward becoming debt-free in a more manageable way.

1. Tally

Tally is an AI-powered app designed specifically for credit card debt. Once you link your credit cards, Tally analyzes the balances, interest rates, and minimum payments on each card. Tally then creates a payment plan to help you minimize interest payments and pay off your debt faster. Tally also offers a line of credit to consolidate your credit card debt, providing a lower interest rate than typical credit cards.

By focusing on high-interest debts first, Tally's AI can create a strategy that saves users money on interest charges, allowing them to pay down debt more efficiently.

Example: According to Tally, users save an average of $5,300 in interest payments over the course of their debt payoff period. Tally's debt management features make it easier for people with high-interest credit card debt to take control and reduce the financial burden.

2. Chime Credit Builder

Chime is a neobank that offers the Chime Credit Builder, a secured credit card designed to help people pay down credit card debt and improve their credit scores. Chime's AI tracks spending and encourages timely payments by offering insights and reminders to keep users on track. While not a debt consolidation tool, Chime Credit Builder can assist users in managing credit responsibly, reducing interest payments, and avoiding future debt.

The card has no fees or interest, and users can set their own limits based on available funds, which means they're less likely to over-spend or accumulate more debt.

Example: Chime reports that many of its users see a positive impact on their credit score after six months of using the Credit Builder account responsibly, which can help reduce debt over time by making it easier to qualify for lower-interest credit in the future.

3. Undebt.it

Undebt.it is a web-based app that uses AI to create personalized debt repayment plans based on your financial situation. You can input your debts, interest rates, and minimum payments, and the platform's algorithms generate an optimized plan to reduce debt efficiently. Users can choose from different debt reduction strategies, such as the "debt snowball" (paying off the smallest balance first) or the "debt avalanche" (paying off the highest-interest debt first).

Undebt.it's AI helps by making calculations for various scenarios, showing how small adjustments can impact your debt payoff timeline. While the basic app is free, it also offers a premium version with extra features like bill reminders and advanced tracking.

Example: Users often find that the debt avalanche method, calculated by Undebt.it, saves more on interest over time than paying debts randomly. By sticking to the recommended plan, many users become debt-free faster than they would with conventional repayment strategies.

4. Credit Karma

Credit Karma is widely known for providing free credit scores and reports, but its AI tools go further by offering personalized insights into debt and credit improvement. Credit Karma's AI analyzes your credit report and gives tailored recommendations for improving your credit score, including strategies to reduce credit card balances and optimize credit utilization.

Credit Karma also provides tools to compare loan consolidation offers. Its AI suggests loans with lower interest rates or better terms, which can be helpful for users looking to consolidate and pay off debt faster.

Example: According to Credit Karma, members who follow their debt payoff and credit improvement recommendations can often see their credit scores rise over several months, which in turn can help reduce the interest rates they qualify for on new credit.

. . .

Key Apps and Services that Automate Debt Payments and Interest Tracking

Staying on top of debt payments, interest tracking, and managing multiple bills can be challenging. AI-powered tools can automate many of these tasks, helping you stay on track with payments, avoid late fees, and minimize interest costs.

1. Prism

Prism is a bill payment app that integrates with over 11,000 billers across the U.S., making it easier to manage all your bills in one place. Once you link your accounts, Prism's AI detects due dates and payment amounts, helping you avoid late fees and stay on top of your obligations. It provides reminders and alerts for upcoming payments, and you can pay bills directly through the app.

Prism's AI even learns your payment behavior, allowing it to predict your cash flow needs and make suggestions about how to optimize payments for better debt management.

Example: Many Prism users report significant reductions in late fees, as the app's reminders and payment organization help them stay on top of their bills, contributing to an improved credit score over time.

2. Qoins

Qoins is a micro-payment app that rounds up everyday purchases and applies the difference toward debt repayment. Qoins' AI tracks your spending, rounding up each transaction and sending the spare change to your creditor. You can set up Qoins to target a specific loan or credit card debt, and it automatically sends payments each month.

This approach is particularly useful for people who want to make progress on their debt without having to budget for larger monthly payments. By rounding up small amounts, Qoins users can gradually pay down their debt without significantly impacting their cash flow.

Example: According to Qoins, users who make regular round-ups and payments through the app pay off their debts about twice as fast as they would with minimum payments alone.

3. Debt Payoff Planner

Debt Payoff Planner is a budgeting app specifically for people focused on reducing debt. It uses AI to create a payment plan based on your debt balances, minimum payments, and interest rates. The app provides visualizations of your debt payoff timeline, helping you stay motivated by tracking your progress.

Debt Payoff Planner offers various repayment methods, including debt snowball and debt avalanche. The app's AI recommends the best method based on your financial goals and updates projections as you make payments.

Example: Users of Debt Payoff Planner often find the debt payoff timeline feature especially motivating, as it shows how long it will take to pay off debt under various scenarios. The app's monthly reports also allow users to celebrate milestones and make adjustments to their strategy as needed.

Final Thoughts: Using AI to Take Control of Bills and Debt

AI-powered tools for bill negotiation, subscription management, and debt reduction can make a significant difference in managing personal finances. By using these tools, you can save money on bills, streamline payments, and reduce debt more efficiently. Whether you're just starting to tackle debt or looking for ways to optimize bill payments, these AI-powered apps can support your financial goals.

AI is making it possible to take control of finances in ways that were previously complex and time-consuming. With these tools, staying on top of bills and debt becomes easier, freeing you to focus on building wealth and achieving financial security.

Quick Start Guide to Lowering Bills and Tackling Debt

Quick Start Guide to Lowering Bills and Tackling Debt

1. **Sign Up for a Bill Negotiation Service**
2. Register with Trim or Rocket Money to have them negotiate bills on your behalf, such as internet, cable, or phone bills.
3. **Connect Your Credit Cards for Automatic Cashback**
4. Use apps like Dosh or Rakuten to maximize cashback on regular purchases, which can go toward debt repayment.
5. **Identify and Prioritize High-Interest Debt**
6. Use an AI-driven tool like Tally to analyze your credit cards and prioritize high-interest debts.
7. **Create a Debt Payment Plan**
8. Follow the recommendations from your app or use a method like the debt snowball (smallest debts first) or avalanche (highest interest first).
9. **Set Up Payment Reminders or Automation**

10. Use bill management apps like Prism to set reminders or automatically pay bills on time, avoiding late fees and interest charges.

Part Four
Growing Wealth with AI Insights

Chapter 10
Building a Diverse Portfolio with AI Assistance

Reminder: For those who indicated an interest in investing or diversifying their portfolio in the Health Check, this chapter will walk you through AI-driven options for building and managing a balanced investment portfolio. We'll cover tools for everything from asset allocation to tracking performance.

Growing wealth isn't just about picking a few good stocks or bonds. True financial growth often requires a diversified portfolio that balances multiple asset classes, like real estate, commodities, and other alternative investments. Fortunately, AI-driven tools now make it easier to diversify effectively, providing insights and automated strategies across a range of asset classes. In this chapter, we'll explore how AI can help you go beyond traditional investments, the benefits of diversification, and tools that simplify and enhance portfolio management.

. . .

How AI Can Help You Diversify Your Portfolio Beyond Stocks and Bonds

Diversification is essential for reducing risk and improving the stability of returns over time. While traditional portfolios often focus on stocks and bonds, today's AI tools allow investors to venture into a wider range of assets without needing in-depth expertise in each area.

1. Alternative Investments with AI Recommendations

AI algorithms can scan the market and identify emerging opportunities in asset classes like real estate, commodities, and even alternative assets like cryptocurrency. These tools analyze patterns, correlations, and risks, allowing investors to make informed choices based on data-driven insights.

For example, tools like **Wealthfront** and **Betterment** offer automated diversification strategies that include international assets, real estate investment trusts (REITs), and even commodities like gold. These platforms utilize AI to optimize the asset mix, balancing the portfolio based on market trends and the user's risk tolerance.

Example: Betterment's AI-driven investment model will automatically adjust the allocation between stocks, bonds, and alternative assets, ensuring that users have exposure to a broad range of assets. This automatic rebalancing keeps the portfolio aligned with the investor's financial goals and market conditions, reducing the need for constant manual adjustments.

2. Balancing Traditional and Alternative Assets

AI tools can also help investors balance traditional and alternative assets. While stocks and bonds remain the backbone of most portfolios, adding assets like real estate or commodities can provide additional protection during market volatility. For instance, commodities tend to have an inverse correlation with stocks, making them a valuable hedge during economic downturns.

Ellevest, a robo-advisor focused on women investors, includes alternative assets like REITs in its portfolios to provide real estate exposure, helping users diversify beyond just stocks and bonds. Its

AI-based algorithms recommend a portfolio allocation based on the investor's specific financial goals, risk tolerance, and timeline.

3. Data-Driven Strategies for Specific Asset Classes

AI can analyze large datasets to reveal insights into the performance of different asset classes, providing data-driven suggestions to diversify and reduce risk. For example, AI algorithms can examine trends in global markets, identify undervalued commodities, or flag specific real estate sectors showing growth potential. This capability enables investors to tap into asset classes they may not have previously considered.

Example: **Zest AI** and other machine-learning platforms provide data analytics services to investment managers, highlighting opportunities across various asset classes. By integrating these insights into personal finance platforms, retail investors can access a wealth of data usually reserved for institutional investors, helping them make well-informed diversification decisions.

AI-Driven Insights on Real Estate, Commodities, and Other Asset Classes

Investing in real estate, commodities, or even private equity can be intimidating without deep industry knowledge. AI simplifies these investment processes by analyzing market trends, identifying opportunities, and providing actionable insights.

1. Real Estate Investment with AI-Driven REITs

Real estate can be a powerful tool for wealth building, but direct real estate investment requires substantial capital and expertise. AI-driven Real Estate Investment Trusts (REITs) make it easier to gain exposure to real estate without the hassle of property ownership. Platforms like **Fundrise** use AI to analyze real estate opportunities and manage REIT portfolios, offering diversified exposure to various properties.

Fundrise's AI algorithms analyze real estate trends and select properties likely to appreciate, generating income through rental yields and asset appreciation. Investors can view detailed data about properties and receive performance projections, helping them make informed decisions without needing expertise in real estate.

Example: Fundrise offers portfolios that include residential, commercial, and industrial properties, with AI recommending allocations based on current market conditions. For instance, if commercial real estate is forecasted to underperform, Fundrise may reduce exposure to that sector and allocate more toward residential or industrial properties.

2. Commodity Investment Platforms

Commodities, such as gold, oil, and agricultural products, can diversify a portfolio by providing a hedge against inflation and market volatility. AI-driven tools analyze historical performance, global market trends, and seasonal patterns in commodities to suggest optimal entry and exit points for investors.

One example is **Goldman Sachs' Marquee platform**, which offers AI-driven insights on commodities. Marquee provides real-time data and predictive models to guide investors on commodity trends, using AI to evaluate global market factors that influence commodity prices. While Goldman Sachs' Marquee is primarily for institutional investors, its predictive analytics and machine learning models represent a shift toward using AI to make commodities more accessible.

For retail investors, apps like **SoFi Invest** allow exposure to commodities through ETFs that track assets like gold and oil. SoFi's AI analyzes risk and performance to recommend diversified ETF portfolios, including commodity ETFs for those looking to hedge against inflation or economic uncertainty.

3. Private Equity and Crowdfunding with AI Insights

Private equity and crowdfunding platforms are typically high-risk but can offer high rewards. AI-based analysis tools assess the potential of startups and private companies, allowing investors to make more informed decisions. **EquityZen**, a marketplace for buying and selling shares of private companies, uses AI to evaluate a company's growth potential, providing investors with insights into pre-IPO opportunities.

Example: EquityZen's AI algorithm considers factors like the company's revenue growth, industry trends, and financial health. While these investments are riskier, the AI-driven data helps investors understand the potential upside and assess whether it aligns with their risk tolerance and diversification strategy.

Tools that Simplify and Enhance the Portfolio Management Process

AI-powered portfolio management tools streamline the complex task of managing multiple asset classes, automating rebalancing, tracking performance, and offering personalized insights. These tools allow investors to stay diversified while keeping an eye on long-term goals.

1. Personal Capital

Personal Capital combines AI-driven insights with traditional financial planning. The app tracks multiple asset classes, including stocks, bonds, REITs, and commodities, and provides real-time insights into portfolio diversification. It also offers a "Retirement Planner" that uses AI to project future needs based on current investments, helping investors make strategic decisions about asset allocation.

Personal Capital's AI algorithms analyze your portfolio against industry benchmarks and suggest changes to balance risk and returns. This feature simplifies diversification, ensuring that your portfolio includes a healthy mix of assets aligned with your financial goals.

Example: Personal Capital may suggest adjusting your exposure to REITs or bonds if you're nearing retirement, helping you reduce risk without compromising long-term growth potential.

2. Schwab Intelligent Portfolios

Schwab Intelligent Portfolios is a robo-advisor that offers AI-driven portfolio management, including a range of asset classes such as international stocks, REITs, and precious metals. The AI-based algorithm diversifies the portfolio according to your financial profile, rebalancing it periodically to maintain your target allocation.

Schwab's platform also provides tax-loss harvesting, which helps offset taxable gains by selling underperforming assets and replacing them with similar investments. This automated feature not only keeps portfolios diversified but also minimizes tax liabilities, which can lead to higher net returns over time.

Example: Schwab's AI-driven rebalancing might adjust your international stock holdings if there's increased volatility, reallocating funds to U.S. stocks or fixed-income assets to stabilize your portfolio.

3. Wealthfront's PassivePlus

Wealthfront's PassivePlus is an AI-powered portfolio management tool that focuses on optimizing returns through strategies like tax-loss harvesting and smart beta. In addition to a diversified range of ETFs, Wealthfront includes alternative investments like REITs and commodities, helping investors achieve broad exposure.

PassivePlus uses AI to monitor the portfolio continuously, making adjustments based on market trends and economic indicators. This proactive approach allows investors to benefit from asset class performance shifts without requiring hands-on management.

Example: Wealthfront's AI might reduce exposure to certain asset classes if a market downturn is expected, minimizing risk and protecting your investment. Wealthfront users can review their portfolios and benefit from automated adjustments that align with their long-term strategy.

4. Betterment's Flexible Portfolios

Betterment's Flexible Portfolios allow investors to customize their allocation across asset classes, from traditional stocks and bonds to international equities and REITs. Betterment's AI-driven platform rebalances portfolios automatically and provides personalized recommendations based on financial goals and market conditions.

The AI engine at Betterment regularly monitors economic indicators, ensuring the portfolio aligns with the investor's risk tolerance and goals. By adjusting allocations as needed, Betterment simplifies the management process while offering diverse investment options.

Example: If Betterment's AI detects high inflation, it may shift part of the portfolio into assets like Treasury Inflation-Protected Securities (TIPS) or commodity ETFs that generally perform well in inflationary environments.

Final Thoughts: The Role of AI in Portfolio Diversification

Diversifying a portfolio with a mix of traditional and alternative assets is one of the best strategies for managing risk and maximizing long-term growth. AI-powered tools have made it easier than ever to achieve this diversification by analyzing trends, providing insights, and automating the portfolio management process.

With AI assistance, investors can explore opportunities across multiple asset classes without needing to be experts in each area. These tools enable investors to build well-rounded portfolios, reduce risk, and stay adaptable as market conditions change. By leveraging AI's analytical power, you can make informed diversification choices and take a proactive approach to wealth-building—one that balances potential returns with a stable, diversified foundation.

Case Study: 55ip's Tax-Smart Investment Strategies

Case Study: 55ip's Tax-Smart Investment Strategies

55ip, founded by Vinay Nair, developed an AI-powered platform offering tax-smart investment strategies through model portfolios. The platform simplifies and enhances the portfolio management process by automating complex tasks, allowing financial advisors to focus on client relationships. This innovation led to 55ip's acquisition by J.P. Morgan Asset Management, highlighting the significant impact of AI in wealth management.

Quick Start Guide to Diversifying Your Investments

Quick Start Guide to Diversifying Your Investments

1. **Choose an AI-Driven Investment Platform**
2. Sign up for a robo-advisor like Betterment or Wealthfront, or a broader portfolio manager like Personal Capital.
3. **Complete a Risk Assessment**
4. Answer questions in the app to assess your risk tolerance and time horizon, so the AI can tailor your portfolio allocation.
5. **Set Your Investment Goals**
6. Use goal-setting features to specify what you're investing for (e.g., retirement, buying a house) and when you plan to achieve it.
7. **Review Suggested Asset Allocation**
8. Explore the AI's recommended mix of assets (stocks, bonds, real estate) and make adjustments if necessary based on your comfort level.

9. **Enable Automatic Rebalancing**

10. Allow the platform to rebalance your portfolio periodically, keeping it aligned with your goals and risk tolerance over time.

Chapter 11

Personalized Financial Advice and Wealth Management

Reminder: If your Health Check pointed to a need for personalized financial advice, this chapter provides insights on how AI-based advisors can offer personalized recommendations, tailored portfolios, and strategies to support your financial growth.

The days of needing to visit a brick-and-mortar office to get financial advice are fading. With the rise of AI-powered "virtual financial advisors," wealth management is becoming more accessible, convenient, and personalized. These digital advisors, backed by powerful algorithms and data, can help manage investments, plan for retirement, and make day-to-day financial decisions with precision. But AI-based financial advice isn't without its limitations, and balancing these insights with traditional guidance can make for a more well-rounded approach to financial health. In this chapter, we'll explore the role of virtual advisors, discuss the benefits and challenges of AI-driven financial guidance, and offer strategies for combining AI with human expertise.

Overview of Virtual Financial Advisors and Their Role in Wealth Management

Virtual financial advisors, also known as robo-advisors or AI-based advisors, are digital platforms that provide automated, algorithm-driven financial planning services. By analyzing vast amounts of data—from market trends to individual spending patterns—AI-based advisors can offer tailored investment and financial advice without the need for direct human involvement.

1. What Virtual Financial Advisors Do

Virtual financial advisors primarily offer services like portfolio management, retirement planning, goal-based investing, and tax optimization. They rely on machine learning algorithms to analyze user data and deliver customized recommendations based on an individual's financial goals, risk tolerance, and time horizon.

For instance, platforms like **Betterment** and **Wealthfront** use AI to assess a client's financial situation and create a portfolio optimized for growth, stability, or income. Users input basic information about their goals, such as saving for retirement or purchasing a home, and the AI-driven advisor generates a plan, allocates assets accordingly, and automatically rebalances as market conditions shift.

2. Features and Services of Virtual Advisors

Virtual advisors offer a range of features that were traditionally available only through human financial advisors:

- **Automated Portfolio Management**: AI-based advisors build and manage portfolios, adjusting asset allocation over time based on market conditions and user goals.

- **Goal-Based Planning**: These platforms support specific financial goals, such as saving for education, retirement, or buying a home, by designing portfolios optimized for each purpose.
- **Tax Optimization**: Many virtual advisors use tax-loss harvesting to offset gains and reduce tax liability. Betterment and Wealthfront are well-known for offering this service as a standard feature.
- **Behavioral Nudges**: Some platforms provide nudges to help users stay disciplined, such as reminding them not to panic-sell during market dips or encouraging contributions to retirement accounts.

The Benefits and Limitations of AI-Based Financial Advice

AI-driven financial advice offers numerous benefits, including accessibility, cost savings, and efficiency. However, it also has limitations, particularly in areas that require nuanced judgment or in-depth knowledge of complex financial situations. Here's a closer look at what AI can—and cannot—do when it comes to financial advice.

Benefits of AI-Based Financial Advice

1. Affordability and Accessibility

One of the most significant benefits of virtual advisors is their affordability. Traditional financial advisors often charge 1-2% of assets under management, while AI-driven platforms like Betterment and Wealthfront typically charge around 0.25% to 0.50%. This makes financial advice accessible to a broader audience, especially those with smaller portfolios who might not meet the minimum requirements for traditional advisory services.

2. Personalization and Precision

AI-driven advisors analyze a user's financial profile, goals, and preferences to provide personalized recommendations. For instance, **Schwab Intelligent Portfolios** uses algorithms to recommend specific asset allocations based on an individual's risk tolerance and financial objectives. By incorporating data and behavioral patterns, virtual advisors can often tailor recommendations with a high degree of precision.

3. Continuous Monitoring and Automated Adjustments

Virtual advisors monitor portfolios 24/7 and can make adjustments based on real-time data. For example, if there's significant market volatility, the AI might rebalance the portfolio to reduce exposure to high-risk assets. This real-time adjustment offers a level of vigilance that human advisors simply cannot match.

4. Behavioral Insights and Discipline

AI advisors are often better than humans at helping clients stay disciplined. For example, when market fluctuations trigger fear, AI advisors can issue reminders about long-term goals, encouraging users to avoid impulsive, emotionally-driven decisions. Platforms like **Personal Capital** provide users with financial planning insights and reminders to stay on track with their goals, helping reduce the risk of costly mistakes.

Limitations of AI-Based Financial Advice

1. Limited Personalization for Complex Situations

While AI can offer precise advice within predefined parameters, it struggles with more complex financial situations. For instance, individuals with unique tax situations, estate planning needs, or non-traditional income sources may find that AI-driven advice lacks the nuance they require. A virtual advisor can't provide guidance on issues like navigating a family business or preparing for retirement with multiple income streams.

2. Lack of Emotional Intelligence

While AI-based advisors excel at data-driven analysis, they can't replicate the human touch. Financial planning is often emotional, involving significant life decisions and personal values. A human advisor can offer empathy, reassurance, and personalized support, which can be critical in times of financial stress or major life transitions, such as marriage, divorce, or inheritance planning.

3. Dependence on User Input

AI-based financial advice is only as accurate as the data provided. If a user inputs inaccurate information about their financial situation, goals, or risk tolerance, the advice generated by the AI may be unsuitable. Traditional advisors are more likely to detect inconsistencies in a financial plan and adjust accordingly, whereas virtual advisors rely solely on user data.

4. Potential for Over-Simplification

AI-driven advice is based on algorithms that simplify complex financial markets, and this can sometimes lead to oversimplified recommendations. For example, an AI-driven advisor might suggest an asset allocation that doesn't fully account for broader economic changes, focusing on past data rather than emerging trends. This can limit the forward-thinking flexibility that human advisors might bring.

Balancing AI Insights with Traditional Financial Guidance

While virtual financial advisors offer valuable support for everyday financial management, complex situations often call for a hybrid approach, combining AI-driven insights with human expertise. Here's how to create a balanced approach.

1. Using AI for Day-to-Day Financial Decisions

For day-to-day financial tasks, such as budgeting, portfolio rebalancing, or goal-based savings, AI-based advisors are highly effective. These tools are designed to handle repetitive tasks, track financial goals, and adjust portfolios without human intervention, making them ideal for routine management.

Example: For someone looking to build a retirement portfolio, a robo-advisor like Wealthfront or Schwab Intelligent Portfolios can provide a straightforward, low-cost approach. The AI handles allocation and rebalancing, so users don't have to worry about monitoring market changes continuously.

2. Engaging a Traditional Financial Advisor for Complex Needs

For more nuanced financial decisions—such as estate planning, major tax events, or managing a large windfall—consulting a human advisor can provide valuable expertise and guidance. Human advisors can offer the emotional intelligence and strategic insight that AI lacks, helping with situations that require a deep understanding of family dynamics, business interests, or tax planning.

Example: If someone inherits a complex portfolio or needs help structuring a business exit, a traditional advisor would be better suited for these complex scenarios. They can develop strategies that take into account tax implications, family trusts, or other specific concerns that virtual advisors aren't equipped to handle.

3. Considering a Hybrid Model with Human-AI Collaboration

Some platforms offer a hybrid model, combining AI-based insights with access to human advisors. For instance, **Betterment Premium** provides automated investment management alongside unlimited access to human financial planners for an additional fee. This setup allows investors to enjoy the cost savings and precision of AI while still having access to personalized advice when needed.

In these hybrid models, the AI handles day-to-day management, while human advisors step in to address more complex questions, review progress toward financial goals, or offer guidance on life transitions.

4. Making Use of Both Tools for Accountability and Clarity

Even if you rely mainly on AI for financial management, a periodic check-in with a traditional advisor can provide additional clarity and accountability. Human advisors can review your financial strategy from an external perspective, offering insight into how your investments align with your life goals, risk tolerance, and personal values.

For instance, meeting with a human advisor annually while using a virtual advisor for daily management can be a balanced approach. The AI takes care of routine tasks, while the human advisor ensures your strategy aligns with broader, long-term objectives.

Final Thoughts: The Evolving Role of AI in Wealth Management

AI-driven financial advice has democratized access to wealth management, making it more affordable, convenient, and data-driven. Virtual advisors excel at managing straightforward financial goals, offering a highly efficient and low-cost way to grow wealth. However, their limitations in complex, emotionally nuanced situations highlight the enduring value of traditional financial guidance.

As AI technology continues to advance, it's likely that virtual advisors will become even more sophisticated, capable of addressing a wider range of financial needs. Yet, the human element in financial planning remains irreplaceable, especially for individuals navigating complex life changes and high-stakes financial decisions.

A balanced approach—leveraging AI for routine management and human expertise for complex needs—offers the best of both worlds. By combining the efficiency and affordability of AI with the insight and empathy of human advisors, investors can build a more resilient and adaptable financial strategy that supports their long-term goals.

Case Study: Upstart Holdings' AI Lending Platform

Case Study: Upstart Holdings' AI Lending Platform

Upstart Holdings, an American financial technology company, utilizes AI to assess creditworthiness by analyzing non-traditional variables such as education and employment. This approach has enabled them to provide consumer loans more effectively, partnering with banks and credit unions to offer personalized lending solutions.

Quick Start Guide to Using AI for Personalized Wealth Management

Quick Start Guide to Using AI for Personalized Wealth Management

1. **Sign Up with a Hybrid Platform**
2. Register with a hybrid platform like Betterment Premium, which offers AI-powered advice and access to human financial advisors.
3. **Connect Financial Accounts for a Full Picture**
4. Connect your accounts to provide the platform with a complete financial picture, which allows for more tailored advice.
5. **Identify Your Primary Goals**
6. Enter your financial goals into the app—such as retirement, saving for education, or wealth growth—so the AI can prioritize advice accordingly.
7. **Schedule a Session with an Advisor**
8. Take advantage of any live advisor sessions included in your platform's plan to discuss any unique needs or concerns.

9. **Set Up Alerts for Financial Milestones**

10. Enable alerts for major milestones or target achievements, such as reaching a savings goal or hitting an investment target.

Chapter 12

Preparing for the Future: Retirement and Long-Term Financial Planning

Reminder: If retirement planning and long-term goals were identified in your DIY Financial Health Check, this chapter is your go-to resource. Here, you'll learn about AI tools that can help forecast retirement savings, assess risks, and create a future-proof plan tailored to your goals.

Retirement and long-term financial planning require careful consideration of goals, risk management, and adaptability. In the past, these tasks required regular meetings with financial advisors and meticulous manual calculations. Today, AI-driven tools make it easier to forecast retirement savings, evaluate risk, and adapt plans to life changes. In this chapter, we'll explore how AI can support retirement and long-term planning by providing data-driven forecasts, assessing risk, and suggesting adaptable strategies that help future-proof your finances.

. . .

Using AI-Driven Tools to Forecast Retirement Savings and Plan for the Future

AI-powered retirement planning tools are changing the way we prepare for the future. These tools use complex algorithms to analyze an individual's savings rate, expected expenses, investment performance, and life expectancy to predict how much money they'll need to retire comfortably. They can also suggest adjustments to savings, investment, and spending habits to improve the likelihood of reaching retirement goals.

1. Forecasting Future Savings Needs

AI-based retirement calculators and financial planning tools can forecast your retirement savings by analyzing your current income, savings rate, and portfolio performance. For example, **Wealthfront** and **Betterment** offer retirement planning tools that use machine learning to simulate different financial scenarios based on user input. They consider factors like inflation, market returns, and potential salary increases to give a more accurate estimate of future retirement savings.

Example: Betterment's "RetireGuide" allows users to input their current savings, age, income, and retirement goals. The tool then uses AI to model the user's portfolio over time, factoring in expected rates of return, inflation, and spending needs. It generates a retirement forecast showing the probability of achieving the desired retirement income and suggests adjustments to savings or investment allocations if the user is at risk of falling short.

2. Personalized Retirement Projections

Personalization is one of the biggest advantages of AI-driven retirement planning tools. Traditional retirement calculators often provide generic results, but AI-powered tools like **Personal Capital** and **Fidelity's Retirement Score** can tailor forecasts based on a wide range of variables, including user behavior and specific spending needs. This level of customization makes it easier to set realistic goals and understand the specific actions required to meet them.

Example: Personal Capital's Retirement Planner not only factors in income, savings rate, and portfolio performance but also allows users to input specific life events like buying a home, sending children to college, or traveling in retirement. The tool's AI uses this data to update retirement projections, showing how each major decision might impact long-term finances.

3. Real-Time Tracking and Adjustments

Some AI-driven platforms, such as **Schwab Intelligent Portfolios** and **Vanguard's Digital Advisor**, allow users to track progress toward retirement goals in real-time. These platforms continuously update based on new data, such as changes in market conditions or adjustments to income, which enables more accurate forecasting. By monitoring your portfolio's performance and updating projections dynamically, AI tools provide users with a constantly refreshed outlook on their retirement readiness.

Example: Schwab Intelligent Portfolios' AI algorithms track market trends and user progress, offering recommendations if the system detects that an individual's current savings or investment strategy may not meet their long-term goals. If market conditions shift significantly, the tool may suggest reallocating assets to maintain progress.

How AI Can Help Assess Risks and Adjust Plans for Changing Life Circumstances

Life is unpredictable, and effective long-term planning must account for unexpected events like job changes, market volatility, health issues, or family responsibilities. AI-powered tools are particularly effective at assessing these risks and providing flexibility to adjust plans as circumstances evolve.

1. Scenario Analysis and Risk Assessment

AI-driven tools can conduct scenario analysis, which allows users to explore different financial outcomes based on varying levels of risk. By simulating market downturns, early retirement, or increased healthcare costs, these tools help users see how potential changes might impact their retirement. For instance, **Vanguard's Digital Advisor** and **Empower**(formerly Personal Capital) offer risk assessment features that show how different levels of market volatility or life events could affect savings goals.

Example: Vanguard's Digital Advisor allows users to test scenarios like "bear markets" or "early retirement." The AI calculates how each scenario might affect retirement savings, providing users with an understanding of potential risks and the opportunity to adjust investment strategies accordingly.

2. Dynamic Rebalancing to Mitigate Risk

AI-based tools not only provide risk assessments but can also automatically rebalance portfolios to reduce exposure to high-risk assets as you approach retirement. This dynamic rebalancing feature, offered by robo-advisors like Betterment and Schwab Intelligent Portfolios, is particularly useful for risk-averse individuals. The AI gradually shifts the portfolio from growth-oriented stocks to more stable assets, like bonds, helping to preserve accumulated wealth and mitigate the risk of major losses close to retirement.

Example: Betterment's algorithms gradually adjust an investor's asset allocation based on proximity to retirement age. As users approach retirement, the AI reduces exposure to volatile assets and increases holdings in more conservative assets like bonds, aiming to protect the portfolio against significant market downturns.

3. Adjusting Plans Based on Life Changes

AI-based tools can also respond to life changes by adjusting retirement plans in real-time. For instance, if a user experiences a significant life event like a job change, an increase in income, or an unexpected expense, AI-driven retirement platforms can update retirement projections accordingly. Tools like **Retirement Planner by Personal Capital**let users input life events, which the AI then incorporates into future projections, adjusting savings recommendations as needed.

Example: If someone receives a promotion or pay raise, Personal

Capital's Retirement Planner allows them to update their income. The AI recalculates retirement projections, suggesting an increase in contributions to keep the user on track for a comfortable retirement.

Future-Proofing Finances Through Evolving Technology and Adaptable Strategies

Preparing for retirement today is not only about planning for the future but also about making sure your financial strategy can adapt as technology and economic conditions change. AI-driven tools are designed to evolve, incorporating new financial products, adapting to changes in market behavior, and helping users stay informed about the best strategies for building long-term financial security.

1. Adapting to Economic and Market Changes

One of AI's greatest strengths is its ability to adapt based on real-time data. Many AI-driven financial planning tools automatically incorporate economic indicators, such as interest rates, inflation, and global market trends, into their algorithms. This responsiveness helps ensure that retirement plans remain relevant and up-to-date, even in changing economic environments.

Example: **Empower's Retirement Planner** adjusts projections based on inflation and changing interest rates, offering recommendations that align with current economic conditions. This ability to adapt to macroeconomic shifts helps users stay on track regardless of market volatility or inflationary pressures.

2. Incorporating New Financial Products and Strategies

As the financial landscape evolves, new products and investment options continue to emerge. AI-driven platforms can integrate these innovations into their recommendations, offering exposure to new asset classes, like sustainable investments or digital assets, as they become more mainstream. By keeping users informed about the latest financial products and opportunities, AI tools help future-proof retirement strategies.

Example: **Schwab Intelligent Portfolios** offers users access to diversified ETFs that include asset classes such as real estate and emerging markets, helping users benefit from these newer investment options as they become available. This adaptability ensures that users have access to a broad range of growth opportunities.

3. Flexible Contribution and Withdrawal Strategies

AI-driven retirement tools also support flexible contribution and withdrawal strategies, which are crucial for long-term planning. Many platforms offer tools that optimize the timing and size of contributions, allowing users to increase or decrease contributions based on current income and expenses. Additionally, some AI-based advisors provide retirement income projections, including safe withdrawal rates and tax-efficient strategies for drawing down funds during retirement.

Example: Betterment's retirement planning tool offers a "Retirement Income" feature that suggests tax-efficient withdrawal strategies, such as drawing from taxable accounts before tax-deferred accounts. This strategy helps users optimize their retirement income while minimizing tax impacts, making funds last longer.

4. Monitoring for Financial Security in Retirement

AI-driven retirement tools are increasingly capable of helping users manage their finances throughout retirement, not just leading up to it. Platforms like **Wealthfront** offer "retirement checkups," where the AI regularly assesses a retiree's financial health, monitoring portfolio performance, cash flow, and potential risks to help retirees stay financially secure.

Example: Wealthfront's retirement checkups evaluate factors like spending patterns, healthcare expenses, and portfolio returns, giving retirees real-time feedback on their spending habits and overall financial health. This ongoing monitoring helps retirees make adjustments as needed to ensure their savings last throughout retirement.

. . .

Final Thoughts: Leveraging AI for a Secure Financial Future

AI-driven tools are revolutionizing retirement and long-term financial planning, offering more accessible, precise, and flexible ways to save and invest for the future. With the ability to forecast savings, assess risks, and adapt plans as life changes, these tools are invaluable for preparing for a financially secure retirement.

However, AI tools should be seen as part of a broader strategy. While they provide robust support for routine planning and adjustments, human oversight is still essential, particularly for complex situations like tax optimization and estate planning. By combining the insights and adaptability of AI with the nuanced judgment of a traditional advisor, individuals can build a well-rounded, resilient financial plan that adjusts to life's inevitable uncertainties.

Future-proofing finances means being proactive, informed, and open to the evolving capabilities of AI-driven financial planning. With the right mix of technology and strategy, you can enjoy greater peace of mind knowing that your retirement and long-term goals are within reach—no matter what the future holds.

Case Study: AZFinText's Predictive Analysis

Case Study: AZFinText's Predictive Analysis

AZFinText, developed by researchers at the University of Arizona, is a textual-based quantitative financial prediction system that uses financial news articles to predict stock price movements. By analyzing breaking financial news and focusing on specific parts of speech, AZFinText achieved a 2.84% trading return over a five-week study period, demonstrating AI's potential in stock market prediction.

Quick Start Guide to AI-Driven Retirement Planning

Quick Start Guide to AI-Driven Retirement Planning

1. **Use an AI-Driven Retirement Calculator**
2. Try the retirement planning tools on apps like Personal Capital, Empower, or Vanguard to project your savings needs.
3. **Enter Detailed Income and Expenses**
4. Add your expected income, contributions, and estimated retirement expenses to get an accurate projection.
5. **Run "What-If" Scenarios**
6. Use your app's scenario analysis to test different life events (early retirement, market downturns) and see how they impact your retirement timeline.
7. **Set Up an Automatic Savings Plan**
8. Automate monthly retirement contributions in an app like Betterment or Wealthfront, ensuring you stay on track.
9. **Revisit and Adjust Annually**

10. Make it a habit to revisit your retirement plan each year and update the information as your situation or goals change.

Part Five

Safeguarding Your AI-Powered Financial Life

Chapter 13
Data Privacy, Security, and Protecting Your Financial Identity

Reminder: If security and privacy were flagged as priorities in your Health Check, this chapter covers essential steps to protect your data while using AI-driven financial tools. Stay vigilant and ensure that your digital financial life is as secure as possible.

The rise of AI-powered financial tools has made managing money more convenient, but it also comes with its own set of risks. From apps that automatically round up your coffee purchase to invest spare change, to robo-advisors that manage your retirement funds, there's a lot of sensitive information involved. With all these handy services analyzing our every dollar, data privacy and security have become major concerns.

In this chapter, we'll dive into the risks of sharing financial data on AI-powered platforms, explore best practices to keep your data secure, and help you protect your financial identity—without needing to resort to a tinfoil hat.

. . .

Risks Associated with Sharing Financial Data in AI-Powered Platforms

When you connect your bank account, credit card, and investment accounts to a financial app, you're sharing more than just numbers. You're entrusting these platforms with your personal information, spending habits, and even your goals. While AI-powered apps often have robust security measures in place, data breaches, privacy concerns, and misuse of data are real risks to consider.

1. Data Breaches and Hacks

Financial data is a prime target for hackers. In recent years, there have been notable breaches that compromised sensitive data, and financial platforms are a tempting target. Even companies with strong security protocols can fall victim to cyber-attacks. When using AI-powered financial tools, it's important to remember that your information could be vulnerable if the platform is hacked.

Example: In 2020, the FinTech platform Dave suffered a data breach that exposed data from 7.5 million users, including names, emails, and some financial details. Though no passwords or financial transaction data were breached, incidents like this highlight the risk of entrusting personal data to online platforms.

2. Data Misuse and Privacy Concerns

AI platforms need access to vast amounts of data to provide personalized financial advice, but there's always the concern of how this data is being used. Some apps may collect more data than necessary and may even use or share it for purposes beyond just managing your finances. Make sure you understand what data is being collected and how it's being used.

Example: Some apps may use your data to target you with personalized ads. While this can seem harmless, the misuse of your spending habits to direct specific ads—or, worse, sell data to third parties—could mean that your financial data is being used for profit without your knowledge.

3. The "All-in-One" Convenience Trade-Off

Many of us appreciate the convenience of having all financial accounts in one app, but it also centralizes a lot of information in one place, increasing the risk if the account is compromised. With a single data breach, a hacker could gain insight into your entire financial profile, including where you shop, your spending habits, and your investment history.

Security Best Practices: Choosing Safe Apps and Services

Despite the risks, there are ways to protect yourself. With the right precautions, you can use AI-powered financial tools without putting your data at unnecessary risk. Here are some best practices to help safeguard your financial life.

1. Choose Reputable Apps and Platforms

Not all financial apps are created equal. Before downloading an app and connecting your bank accounts, do some research. Reputable apps are transparent about their data security policies and often go through rigorous audits to ensure they're protecting your data.

How to Choose: Look for apps from well-established companies or those that are endorsed by major financial institutions. Check if the platform is SOC 2 (Service Organization Control 2) certified, which indicates that it follows strict standards for data security.

2. Read the Privacy Policy (Yes, Really)

We know: privacy policies are boring, but they're also the best way to understand how your data is used and stored. Find out if the app shares data with third parties, what type of information it collects, and how long it keeps your data on file.

Quick Tip: Look for apps that explicitly state they won't sell or share your data with third parties. Some apps, like **Mint**and **Personal Capital**, state that while they may share data internally, they don't sell it to outside companies for advertising.

3. Enable Two-Factor Authentication (2FA)

Two-factor authentication adds an extra layer of protection by requiring you to verify your identity through a second method, such as a text message code or an authentication app. Enabling 2FA is one of the simplest and most effective ways to protect your accounts from unauthorized access.

Example: Financial apps like **Betterment** and **Wealthfront** support 2FA, requiring a unique code from your phone in addition to your password. This ensures that even if your password is compromised, a hacker would need access to your phone to get into your account.

4. Use Strong, Unique Passwords for Each App

It's tempting to reuse the same password across multiple accounts, but this creates a significant security risk. If one account is compromised, all of your accounts using the same password are also vulnerable. Using strong, unique passwords for each financial app can help minimize this risk.

Password Tips: Use a combination of uppercase and lowercase letters, numbers, and symbols, and avoid anything easy to guess, like "password123" or "MySavings." Consider using a password manager to securely store and generate strong passwords for you.

5. Regularly Review Account Activity

Even with strong security measures in place, it's a good idea to check your account activity regularly for any unusual transactions. Most apps offer real-time notifications for transactions, helping you spot unauthorized activity immediately.

Example: Many AI-powered apps, such as **Truebill (Rocket Money)** and **Trim**, can send alerts for unusual spending activity or higher-than-usual bills. This feature helps users catch suspicious activity before it becomes a serious problem.

6. Limit Data Access Permissions

When connecting financial accounts, apps often request permission to access a variety of data points. Only grant access to what's necessary for the app to function. For example, if you're using a budgeting app, it likely doesn't need access to your entire transaction history, just specific categories.

Example: On platforms like **Plaid** (a service that many financial apps use to link bank accounts), users can often manage and revoke permissions as needed. Review these permissions periodically to ensure the app only has access to what's necessary.

7. Be Wary of Phishing Attacks

Phishing attacks, where hackers send fake messages to trick you into sharing personal information, are still one of the most common ways financial accounts are compromised. Be cautious about clicking links or providing login information in response to unsolicited messages. Financial apps and institutions will never ask for sensitive information via email.

Quick Tip: If you receive an email or text asking you to log into a financial app, go directly to the app or website instead of clicking on the link. This simple step can help prevent you from falling victim to phishing schemes.

Protecting Your Financial Identity: Going Beyond the Basics

In addition to these best practices, there are a few advanced steps you can take to further protect your financial identity.

1. Monitor Your Credit Regularly

Monitoring your credit is an effective way to catch any suspicious activity, such as new accounts opened in your name. Services like **Credit Karma** and **Experian** offer free credit monitoring and will alert you to changes in your credit report, allowing you to take immediate action if something looks off.

Example: If you receive an alert that a new account was opened, but you didn't initiate it, you can place a fraud alert on your credit file or even freeze your credit to prevent further unauthorized activity.

2. Consider Identity Theft Protection Services

For added peace of mind, consider signing up for an identity theft protection service. Companies like **LifeLock** and **IdentityForce** offer credit monitoring, identity restoration, and fraud insurance. These services monitor for signs of identity theft across multiple channels, including bank accounts, social media, and the dark web.

Example: IdentityForce, for instance, scans black-market sites and data breach forums to check if your personal information has been exposed, helping you take action quickly in the event of a security breach.

3. Opt for Biometric Authentication if Available

Many apps now offer biometric authentication, such as fingerprint or facial recognition, which adds another layer of security. This option is more secure than traditional passwords and ensures that only you can access your account. AI-driven platforms like **Chime** and **Robinhood** offer biometric login options on mobile devices.

Example: Facial recognition on apps like Robinhood allows only the authorized user to access their account. Biometric data is stored locally on the device rather than on servers, which adds an additional layer of security against breaches.

Final Thoughts: Staying Safe While Leveraging AI-Powered Financial Tools

AI-powered financial tools offer tremendous convenience and insights, but data privacy and security must remain top priorities. As a rule of thumb, approach financial apps with caution, choose reputable platforms, and take advantage of security features like two-factor authentication and biometric login.

Remember that while technology can simplify managing your finances, it's essential to keep your data secure and monitor activity regularly. By following these best practices, you can safely enjoy the benefits of AI-driven financial tools without compromising your privacy or security. So go ahead, let AI help you manage your money —just keep those digital doors securely locked.

Case Study: Mint's Overdraft Early Warning System (ODEWS)

Case Study: Mint's Overdraft Early Warning System (ODEWS)

Mint, a personal finance app, implemented an AI-driven Overdraft Early Warning System (ODEWS) to help users avoid overdraft fees. By analyzing users' banking and transaction data, ODEWS assesses the risk of overdrafting within the next week and sends alerts to at-risk customers. This system resulted in a $3 million savings in overdraft fees for Mint customers compared to a control group.

Quick Start Guide to Staying Safe with Financial AI Tools

Quick Start Guide to Staying Safe with Financial AI Tools

1. **Enable Two-Factor Authentication (2FA)**
2. Turn on 2FA for all your financial apps to add an extra layer of security beyond just your password.
3. **Use Strong, Unique Passwords**
4. Use a password manager to generate and store unique, strong passwords for each account, avoiding reuse.
5. **Review App Permissions**
6. Double-check permissions for each app and limit access to only the necessary accounts and data.
7. **Sign Up for Credit Monitoring**
8. Use a free service like Credit Karma to monitor your credit and receive alerts about any suspicious activity.
9. **Familiarize Yourself with the App's Privacy Policy**
10. Review the privacy policy of each app to understand how your data is used and ensure it aligns with your comfort level.

Chapter 14

Chapter 14: Ethical and Social Implications of AI in Finance

Reminder: If ethical and social considerations are important to you, revisit your Health Check to see if there are AI-driven tools you may want to reevaluate based on ethical considerations. This chapter will help you think about values and align your financial choices accordingly.

AI is transforming personal finance, making financial planning, investing, and money management more accessible. But with these advances come significant ethical and social considerations. AI has the power to influence who has access to financial resources, which can impact economic equality. It also raises questions about privacy, bias, and the role of technology in personal decisions. In this chapter, we'll explore how AI shapes financial access, examine the ethical debates surrounding AI in personal finance, and consider how to choose tools and platforms that align with your values.

. . .

How AI Shapes Financial Access and Equality – The Benefits and Concerns

AI's impact on financial access is both promising and complex. On one hand, AI-driven tools are democratizing finance, making resources like investment advice, budgeting help, and credit assessments more available to a broader audience. On the other hand, concerns about algorithmic bias, data privacy, and digital exclusion raise questions about AI's role in fostering financial equality.

1. Increased Accessibility to Financial Services

One of AI's greatest strengths is its ability to provide financial resources to people who were previously underserved or excluded by traditional finance. AI-driven tools often come with low fees, lower minimum requirements, and automated processes that reduce the need for human intervention. These features make banking, investing, and financial advice more accessible to young people, low-income individuals, and those with limited financial literacy.

Example: Robo-advisors like **Betterment** and **Wealthfront** have reduced the minimum investment required to get started. Where traditional financial advisors may have required substantial starting capital, robo-advisors typically require no minimum deposit or just a few hundred dollars, making investing more accessible to everyday people.

2. Potential for Algorithmic Bias

While AI's accessibility can benefit many, it also introduces the potential for algorithmic bias. AI algorithms are trained on historical data, which can reflect societal inequalities and biases. For instance, if a credit-scoring AI is trained on historical loan data that favored higher-income, white applicants, the algorithm might unwittingly perpetuate this bias, making it harder for marginalized groups to access credit.

Example: In 2019, Apple's **Apple Card**, issued by Goldman Sachs, came under fire when reports surfaced that the algorithm gave lower credit limits to women compared to men, even when they had similar financial profiles. Although unintended, this bias highlighted the risk of AI perpetuating historical inequalities in credit scoring.

3. Digital Divide and Access Inequality

While AI-driven financial tools are more accessible, they are largely digital, which can create a barrier for those without reliable internet access or smartphones. This "digital divide" means that some communities may be excluded from the benefits of AI-powered financial tools, often reinforcing existing inequalities. According to a 2021 Pew Research study, 15% of adults in the U.S. do not have access to a smartphone, with higher rates of digital exclusion among low-income households and rural communities.

Increased reliance on digital platforms for finance could exacerbate disparities if these groups are left out. Financial institutions and AI providers need to address this digital divide to ensure AI benefits reach all segments of society.

Understanding the Ethical Debates Around AI in Personal Finance

AI in personal finance brings up ethical issues about privacy, autonomy, and accountability. Understanding these debates is essential to navigate the AI-powered financial landscape responsibly.

1. Privacy and Data Security

AI-powered financial tools need vast amounts of data to function effectively, which raises concerns about privacy. Many apps require access to sensitive information like spending patterns, income, and credit history. This data, when processed by AI, can help create accurate financial recommendations but also introduces a privacy risk if the data is misused, mishandled, or sold to third parties.

Example: In 2020, **Plaid**, a service that links user bank accounts to apps like Venmo and Robinhood, settled a privacy lawsuit for $58 million after accusations that it had collected more data than necessary. This highlighted the potential risks of giving financial apps unrestricted access to personal data.

2. Transparency and Accountability

AI algorithms are often opaque, meaning users may not fully understand how decisions are being made. This "black box" problem can be problematic, especially when it impacts personal finance. For instance, if an AI denies someone a loan, the applicant might not know why, making it difficult to contest the decision. Transparency and accountability in AI models are crucial for fairness and trust.

Example: Many credit-scoring algorithms used by financial institutions are proprietary, meaning they aren't required to disclose how scores are calculated. If a user's loan is denied or their credit limit reduced due to an AI decision, the lack of transparency makes it difficult to challenge or understand the reasoning behind it.

3. Autonomy and Consumer Choice

While AI tools can simplify financial management, there's a risk that people may become overly reliant on automated recommendations, losing the ability to make independent financial choices. As AI becomes more integrated, it's crucial to strike a balance between AI recommendations and personal judgment, ensuring users retain autonomy over their finances.

Example: Some budgeting apps automatically categorize spending and suggest limits for each category. While helpful, these suggestions may inadvertently shape a user's spending habits, even if they don't align with their personal priorities. Users should be aware of this influence and stay actively involved in their financial decisions.

4. Ethical Use of Financial Data

There are ethical considerations around how AI companies use financial data. Some platforms monetize user data by selling insights to third parties or advertising products, which can raise conflicts of interest. It's essential to evaluate how companies use data and ensure they prioritize user welfare over profit.

Example: Many free financial apps generate revenue by promoting credit cards, loans, or other financial products based on user data. While these suggestions can be beneficial, they may sometimes prioritize profits over the user's financial health, pushing products with high interest rates or fees that may not align with the user's best interests.

The Importance of Choosing Tools and Platforms That Align with Personal Values

With numerous AI-driven financial platforms available, it's increasingly important to choose tools that align with your values. This involves assessing how a company handles data privacy, ethical practices, and social responsibility.

1. Prioritize Platforms with Transparent Data Policies

When choosing an AI-powered financial tool, look for platforms that clearly state how they collect, use, and protect your data. Reputable apps will outline their data-sharing policies and won't sell your data to third parties without explicit consent. Opting for transparency not only protects your privacy but also supports companies that respect user rights.

Example: Some apps, like **Chime** and **Personal Capital**, have privacy policies that explicitly state they do not sell user data to third parties. Users can be confident that these companies prioritize data protection over monetization.

2. Consider Ethical and Social Impact

Certain AI platforms focus on ethical investing or provide services with a social impact. For instance, some robo-advisors offer socially responsible investment (SRI) portfolios, which align investments with values like environmental sustainability or gender equality. Choosing an AI-powered advisor that aligns with your personal values can help you make a positive impact while growing your wealth.

Example: **Ellevest**, a robo-advisor geared towards women, offers socially responsible investment options that support companies with high ratings in gender equity and sustainable practices. Choosing tools like Ellevest allows users to invest in a way that aligns with their personal ethics.

3. Support Platforms Committed to Reducing Algorithmic Bias

Some companies are actively working to reduce bias in their algorithms, promoting fairness in credit assessments, loan approvals, and other financial decisions. Supporting platforms that prioritize fairness and inclusivity helps ensure that AI-powered finance benefits a broader spectrum of people.

Example: Fintech companies like **Petal** have developed alternative credit-scoring models that use cash flow instead of traditional credit scores to evaluate an applicant's creditworthiness. This approach helps improve access to credit for people without an extensive credit history, reducing bias against those who may have been excluded by conventional scoring methods.

4. Stay Informed and Advocate for Ethical Standards

AI-powered financial tools are constantly evolving, and new ethical challenges continue to emerge. Staying informed about these developments empowers you to make responsible choices and advocate for greater accountability. As AI becomes more integral to finance, users have the power to influence companies by choosing platforms that uphold ethical practices and holding those that don't accountable.

Example: When the controversy around Apple Card's gender bias surfaced, public pressure led to increased scrutiny on how algorithms make credit decisions. By being proactive and vocal about ethical standards, users can encourage financial institutions to adopt fairer, more transparent AI practices.

Final Thoughts: Navigating the Ethical Landscape of AI in Personal Finance

The convenience and accessibility of AI-powered financial tools are undeniable, but it's essential to remain mindful of the ethical implications. From issues around privacy and data security to questions of bias and transparency, the ethical landscape of AI in personal finance is complex and evolving. Making informed choices about which platforms to use—and holding them accountable—empowers users to benefit from AI without compromising their values.

Choosing tools that align with your ethics, staying informed, and advocating for responsible practices allows you to harness the benefits of AI while contributing to a fairer, more inclusive financial future. As AI continues to shape personal finance, responsible and informed use can help create a financial landscape that serves all users more equitably.

Quick Start Guide to Choosing Ethical AI Financial Tools

Quick Start Guide to Choosing Ethical AI Financial Tools

1. **Research the Company's Data Usage and Privacy Policies**
2. Before committing to a platform, check how it handles user data and look for transparency on data-sharing practices.
3. **Choose Tools that Support Socially Responsible Investing (SRI)**
4. If values-based investing is important to you, use apps like Ellevest or Wealthsimple, which offer SRI portfolios aligned with ethical practices.
5. **Look for Platforms Committed to Fairness**
6. Support platforms like Petal that prioritize inclusivity by using alternative credit-scoring models to reduce bias.
7. **Stay Updated on Ethical Fintech Trends**
8. Follow news outlets or blogs covering fintech ethics and AI transparency to keep up with the latest developments.

9. **Take a Personal "Values Audit" of Your Finances**

10. Reflect on what financial practices align with your values and use this audit to guide your choices in selecting AI tools.

Afterword: Navigating the Future of Money in an AI-Driven World

Congratulations! If you've made it this far, you're now the proud owner of a mental toolbox filled with AI-powered financial strategies, budgeting apps, robo-advisors, and security tips. You've journeyed through the good, the bad, and the downright sci-fi side of AI in personal finance, and—unlike your wallet—you're much richer for it. But here's the twist: as quickly as you've absorbed these insights, the world of fintech is already brewing up new innovations to keep you on your toes.

AI is Your Partner, Not Your Pilot

First things first—never let an app tell you how to feel about your finances. Remember, AI is here to serve you, not replace your judgment. Just because your robo-advisor suggests investing in something doesn't mean it's a green light to close your eyes and hope for the best. Technology can be brilliant at handling data, crunching numbers, and spotting patterns, but it doesn't know that you love lattes or that you're saving up for an alpaca farm. Keep your goals at the forefront and think of AI as your friendly, if somewhat nerdy, sidekick—not the hero of your financial story.

Keep the Learning Going: Fintech's Not Slowing Down

AI in finance is advancing faster than my morning coffee addiction. Staying informed is no longer a nice-to-have; it's essential. New tools, apps, and algorithms are popping up constantly, each one promising to be "the next big thing." And while some are, others... not so much. By staying curious and updated, you'll know which tech trends are worth your time and which ones are just shiny distractions.

Here are a few easy ways to stay sharp in the world of fintech:

1. **Follow Trusted Financial News Sources**: Outlets like **Bloomberg**, **The Wall Street Journal**, and **Forbes** have entire sections dedicated to fintech and AI. If there's a major development in AI-driven finance, you can bet they're covering it.

2. **Explore Fintech Blogs and Podcasts**: Blogs like **Finextra** and **TechCrunch** or podcasts like **Fintech Insider** offer easy-to-digest insights on fintech trends, straight from experts (and often with a healthy dose of humor).

3. **Take Online Courses**: Websites like **Coursera** and **Udemy** offer courses on fintech and AI, from beginner to advanced. These are great resources if you're curious to dig deeper or need a little help decoding some of the AI lingo.

A Final Word on Balance: Robots Don't Have Bank Accounts

AI may be good at managing money, but it's still a few paychecks away from paying for a round at happy hour. So as you continue exploring these tools, remember that personal finance is exactly that—personal. You're the only one who can decide what makes you feel financially secure, how much you're willing to invest, and what gives you peace of mind. Use AI to enhance your decisions, but keep a firm hand on the wheel. Remember, AI can calculate risk, but only you can decide what's worth it.

And don't be afraid to ask questions! "How does this work?" "Where does my data go?" "Are you *sure* this algorithm won't empty my bank account?" The future belongs to those who embrace curiosity, after all.

Embrace the Future, But Keep It Real

As we wrap up this journey, know this: the future of finance is exciting, a little weird, and very much driven by technology. But as tech reshapes the financial landscape, you have the power to stay informed, stay safe, and stay in charge. Embrace the wonders AI has to offer, but remember to keep it grounded in your values, your goals, and your gut instincts.

The road ahead is full of new fintech twists and AI innovations that will make managing money easier, faster, and sometimes downright magical. But no matter how sophisticated our tools become, nothing can replace good old-fashioned financial savvy, a willingness to learn, and a dash of common sense. Here's to your journey into the future of money—keep learning, keep adapting, and remember, AI is powerful, but your choices are priceless.

Appendices

Here's a final boost to help you navigate the world of AI-powered personal finance! These appendices provide additional resources, a glossary of must-know terms, and recommended reading and learning resources to keep you informed and ready to take on the ever-evolving fintech landscape.

Appendix A: Recommended Tools & Resources

A list of popular AI-driven financial tools, apps, and websites for you to explore:

Budgeting & Expense Tracking

- **Mint** – A classic and powerful budgeting app that categorizes spending and provides AI-powered insights.
- **You Need a Budget (YNAB)** – Helps users build disciplined budgets and tracks progress toward financial goals.
- **PocketGuard** – Shows a real-time "safe-to-spend" amount and manages bills and subscriptions.

Investment & Portfolio Management

- **Betterment** – A robo-advisor that offers diversified portfolios, tax optimization, and financial planning.
- **Wealthfront** – Offers automated portfolio management with additional services like financial goal planning.
- **Schwab Intelligent Portfolios** – Combines AI-driven portfolio management with low fees and a range of asset classes.

Retirement Planning

- **Personal Capital** – Free financial tracking and paid advisory services for retirement planning and investment.
- **Empower Retirement** – Tools and resources for retirement planning and personalized advice.

Debt Management

- **Tally** – AI-driven tool to consolidate credit card debt and lower interest payments.

- **Qoins** – Rounds up daily purchases to pay off debt, working as an effortless debt-reduction tool.

Bill Management & Subscription Management

- **Trim** – Analyzes and negotiates bills, cancels unwanted subscriptions, and helps users save money.
- **Rocket Money (formerly Truebill)** – Tracks and manages subscriptions and negotiates bills for users.

Credit Monitoring & Identity Protection

- **Credit Karma** – Free credit monitoring with AI-driven insights into credit score improvements.
- **Experian** – Provides real-time alerts, credit score tracking, and identity theft protection.
- **LifeLock** – Offers identity theft monitoring, credit monitoring, and identity restoration services.

Appendix B: Glossary of Terms

A quick-reference guide to AI, finance, and tech-related terms:

- **Algorithm**: A set of rules or calculations a computer follows to solve problems or complete tasks.
- **Alternative Investments**: Investments beyond stocks and bonds, including real estate, commodities, and private equity.
- **Artificial Intelligence (AI)**: The simulation of human intelligence by computers, enabling them to perform tasks that typically require human intelligence.
- **Augmented Reality (AR)**: Technology that overlays digital elements (like images or sounds) onto the real world.
- **Asset Allocation**: The process of dividing investments among different asset classes to balance risk and reward.
- **Biometric Authentication**: Security process using unique biological characteristics, like fingerprints or facial recognition, for identity verification.
- **Blockchain**: A decentralized digital ledger that records transactions across many computers, used commonly for cryptocurrencies.
- **Digital Wallet**: An electronic device or service that stores payment information for various payment methods, often accessed via smartphone.
- **Machine Learning (ML)**: A branch of AI where algorithms improve over time by learning from data, without explicit programming.
- **Phishing**: A type of online scam where attackers pose as legitimate entities to steal personal information.
- **Rebalancing**: Adjusting a portfolio's asset mix to maintain its target allocation, often automated in robo-advisors.

- **Robo-Advisor**: An automated, algorithm-based investment platform that provides financial planning services with minimal human intervention.
- **Tax-Loss Harvesting**: Selling investments at a loss to offset gains and reduce taxable income.
- **Two-Factor Authentication (2FA)**: A security measure requiring two forms of identification to access an account, such as a password and a one-time code.

Appendix C: Further Reading and Learning Resources

Books, blogs, and courses to deepen your understanding of AI, finance, and fintech:

Books

- *AI Superpowers: China, Silicon Valley, and the New World Order* by Kai-Fu Lee – A look at the global impact of AI, including its economic and financial implications.
- *Life After Google: The Fall of Big Data and the Rise of the Blockchain Economy* by George Gilder – Explores blockchain, digital finance, and the changing economy.
- *The Simple Path to Wealth* by JL Collins – A practical guide to building wealth and managing investments, with easy-to-understand strategies.

Blogs and Websites

- **Finextra** – News and research on fintech trends, AI in finance, and emerging technologies.
- **TechCrunch Fintech Section** – Covers the latest updates on AI-driven finance tools and industry innovations.
- **NerdWallet** – Offers resources, comparisons, and advice on a range of personal finance topics, from credit scores to retirement planning.

Online Courses

- **Coursera: AI for Everyone by Andrew Ng** – Introductory course on the basics of AI, its applications, and its impact across industries, including finance.
- **Udemy: Fintech and Digital Finance Essentials** – A course that covers digital transformation in finance, AI applications, and the fintech ecosystem.

- **edX: Principles of Machine Learning** – Learn
  the fundamentals of machine learning and how it's
  applied in areas like personal finance.

These appendices are here to keep you informed, inspired, and ready
to take control of your finances with confidence. Explore these
resources, expand your knowledge, and remember: the more you
know, the better equipped you'll be to navigate the AI-driven world
of finance.